CONFESSIONS OF A GHOSTWRITER

ANDREW CROFTS

ISIS
LARGE
PRINT

First published in Great Britain 2014
by
The Friday Project
An imprint of HarperCollins*Publishers*

First Isis Edition
published 2017
by arrangement with
HarperCollins*Publishers*

A catalogue record for this book is available
from the British Library.

ISBN 978–1–78541–316–2 (hb)
ISBN 978–1–78541–322–3 (pb)

Published by
F. A. Thorpe (Publishing)
Anstey, Leicestershire

Set by Words & Graphics Ltd.
Anstey, Leicestershire
Printed and bound in Great Britain by
T. J. International Ltd., Padstow, Cornwall

This book is printed on acid-free paper

Disclaimer

The events described in this book are based on my experiences as a ghostwriter. For reasons of privacy and client confidentiality I have made certain adjustments, altering identifying features and fictionalising some aspects, but it remains an honest reflection of my life.

To my wife, Susan, who I love with all my heart.

Introduction

"Ghostwriter for Hire"

I placed the small ad in *The Bookseller*, a publishing trade magazine, simply adding my phone number, and over the following years those three words took me all over the globe.

They allowed me to meet people I would otherwise never have known existed and who would reveal to me the secrets of their worlds. I travelled from palaces to brothels, lush jungles to mean city streets and got behind the closed doors of both corporate boardrooms and the homes of dysfunctional families.

Hiding behind the title of ghostwriter I could converse with kings and billionaires as easily as whores and the homeless; go backstage with rock stars and actors and descend into the bowels of the earth with miners and engineers. I could stick my nose into everyone else's business and ask all the impertinent questions I wanted to. At the same time I could also live the pleasant life of a writer, my days unencumbered by hours of crowded commuting or unnecessary meetings in bleakly lit offices with people who were of no interest.

I had accidentally stumbled upon a path that was paved with a constant stream of adventures and the following are some of my confessions from along that path.

An eight-foot transsexual hooker in the living room

I was having a well-earned afternoon powernap at the end of a hard working week when my wife came into the bedroom with disturbing news.

"There's an eight-foot transsexual hooker in the living room," she said without even bothering to check if I was still sleeping. "I think you should come down."

"In the living room?" I wasn't entirely sure if I was awake or still dreaming. "How did she get there?"

"She arrived in a taxi. Didn't you hear it?"

"I think I was asleep." I hauled myself up into a sitting position as my wife attempted to flatten my bed-hair. "Is it Geraldine?"

"Obviously."

"What's she doing down here?"

"At the moment she's playing Barbies with the girls, but I think it's you she's come to see."

"Did you talk to her?"

"Of course I talked to her. You weren't there and the girls had an attack of shyness. She's very big and she's wearing a full-length fur coat. They thought she was Cruella de Vil."

"She's fun, isn't she?" I stood up, my head clearing. "I told you."

My wife was exaggerating. Geraldine wasn't anything close to eight feet tall. Without her heels I doubt that she was much more than six feet two or three. But then she did always tend to wear boots with stacked heels and liked to pile her wigs high. By the time I got downstairs the girls had spread their entire collection of Barbies out for inspection across the carpet in front of her shiny white boots and she had shrugged the fur coat down off her shoulders like she was Ava Gardner at a press conference in Cannes. I noticed there was an overnight bag beside her chair.

"Did you get my message?" she asked.

"Message?"

"I left a telephone message to say I had to see you. We need to do some serious rewrites."

"Rewrites?" This was the first I'd heard of this. "But the publisher has signed off on the manuscript. They're happy with everything."

"But it's not right. I need to change things. It's not printed is it?"

"I have no idea, but I doubt they will want to make any more changes now."

That was the moment when Geraldine started to cry and my wife managed to tear the wide-eyed, open-mouthed girls away from the show and into the kitchen to make tea. I felt a bit like crying myself. One of the best moments in the book-writing business is the

4

one when the editor accepts the final version of the typescript and agrees to send it off to the printers. The weight of months of work and uncertainty lifts from your shoulders and there is a brief period of elation (not to mention a cheque in the post) before you have to start worrying about whether the shops are going to display the book, the papers are going to review it and the public are going to buy it. Geraldine's panic was crushing my moment.

I had got to know her well enough over the months to be aware that if she had decided on a course of action she would not be easily diverted; going on the game and changing your gender are both decisions that require uncommon degrees of grit and character. It seemed best to go with the flow for the moment, at least until she had calmed down a bit.

"Are you wanting to work on it over the weekend?" I asked, casting a quizzical look at the overnight bag.

"Yes," she said, "we have to. I'll need to find a bed-and-breakfast or something so we can work during the day."

"Don't be silly," my wife interrupted from the door, the girls peering round her skirts, "you can stay here. We've got a spare room."

Maybe it's something to do with female instincts, but as usual she was ahead of me in reading the situation. Geraldine did not want to rewrite the book any more than I did. There had to be some other reason for her arrival out of the blue at the other end of the country from the streets and kerbs where she plied her trade, and we just had to wait for it to emerge. As she relaxed

5

into the evening, with the help of a bottle of wine, she opened up with a new story about a murderous pimp who she had thought was the love of her life but who was actually making her life a misery. He had arranged for her to be evicted from her flat and was now pursuing her with a gun.

"Sounds like you've got a sequel to your book," my wife suggested as we washed up after sending an exhausted Geraldine up to bed, which was a relief since we'd signed a two-book deal with the publisher and finding enough material for follow-ups was nearly always an uphill struggle. It may be true that "everyone has a book in them", but most people definitely do not have two, however much the publisher's accounting and sales departments may hope to the contrary.

A million books in an African warehouse

"You must fly down for the launch of the book," the Minister boomed, "I insist. The President will be there. It will be a great day. There will be food and speeches. I will make all the arrangements for you."

I didn't really want to go, but there was no arguing with him. Most clients don't even admit that they've used a ghostwriter; they certainly don't want to invite him or her half way across the world to the launch party. In most cases they don't even let the ghost know that there is going to be a party. Once the book is written and delivered the ghost normally slinks back into the shadows and moves on to the next project, allowing the client to bask in the glory of being a published author. The Minister, however, was a man who enjoyed the limelight so much he wanted to share it with the whole world, which was one of the reasons he was such an endearing man.

His extremely efficient assistant made the arrangements through the embassy in London and a business class ticket was delivered to the house by a driver. I didn't even bother to ask about accommodation arrangements because my previous trips had shown that the Minister was the most hospitable of men. He would have thought of everything. Often when you arrive at the borders of a country other than your own you need to provide evidence of where you will be staying. When your ticket has been arranged by someone like the Minister everything is different. Someone would have had a word in the ear of the airport officials, money or other favours would have been exchanged, minders would be waiting to take me to an SUV with darkened windows. It had happened like that every time I had been to see him during the writing process.

The launch of the book was held in a government office that I hadn't been to before. The building must have been designed in colonial times and had a suitable air of faded grandeur, befitting a distinguished literary event. A feast had been laid out for guests on trestle tables and groups of sofas and armchairs had been clustered around the room so that politicians and business people could huddle and whisper, their conspiratorial conversations occasionally interrupted with roars of laughter and outbreaks of back-slapping. There were surprisingly large piles of books which the guests were helping themselves to, flicking through the pages in search of their own names or those of their rivals.

The arrival of the President momentarily overshadowed the Minister's flamboyant act as host and newly published author. The pecking order took a few moments to readjust before everyone was comfortable once more.

The Minister made a speech and graciously acknowledged his ghostwriter in a remarkable display of modesty, honesty and openness. The President also made a speech praising the Minister. Conversations then resumed as one politician after another stood to tell the room how much they admired the author of the book and how exciting it was that his ideas on how to lead Africa to future prosperity were now set down in print.

The Minister smiled and nodded his appreciation to each of the speakers in turn, but he was also working the room as they talked, shaking hands and hugging everyone who came near him.

As he moved closer to where I was standing I overheard him accepting praise from a woman swathed in colourful traditional dress, a Rolex glinting on her wrist.

"Your book will be a bestseller," she assured him.

"Yes, yes," he grinned his acknowledgement, "we have a million copies printed up and ready to distribute. We want every child in Africa to have a copy."

I caught his eye over the lady's shoulder and smiled. I knew that it was his knack for positive thinking and dreaming big dreams that had got him where he was and might yet get him into the presidential palace. The book, I knew, was just one more step in the process of establishing himself as a future leader. Eventually he reached me and clapped a mighty arm around my shoulder.

"Are you having a good time, my friend?" he asked. "Are you glad that you came?"

"Yes, very good," I said. "How many copies have you actually had printed?"

"A million," he said as if it were the most obvious thing in the world.

"I thought we'd agreed to start with a couple of thousand," I said, still not sure whether to believe the bombast.

"You know me," he winked, "I like to think big. I believe in the message of the book. I want copies in every school in Africa."

"You've actually had a million copies printed?"

I was trying to imagine what a million copies of a book must look like. Even if he was exaggerating and he had only printed a tenth of that figure it would still mean crates and crates of books.

"Yes, of course."

"Where are they?"

"My brother has a warehouse near to the town where my mother lives. You remember going there?"

"Of course."

I had spent a pleasant weekend with his mother, a sunny, smiling woman who spoke no English and passed her days happily sitting in the shade inside the walls of the family compound, preparing food to be cooked by her daughters and shouting abuse at the goats whenever they strayed amongst her vegetables. I could imagine the delivery lorries arriving in the tiny town, coating the watching locals with dust from the unmade roads. In his home area the Minister was like a king and the warehouse full of books would be one more jewel in the crown of his glorious career.

As far as I know the crates are still in the warehouse.

Discovering ghostwriting

My first invitation to ghostwrite came from a management guru I was interviewing for *Director* magazine, the house journal for the Institute of Directors, which is a sort of gentlemen's club for business people housed in one of those grand buildings in Pall Mall.

The guru and I were driving back to his gleaming white Surrey mansion in his powder blue Rolls Royce, having had a very long lunch and feeling exceedingly mellow.

"You're a writer," he said, apropos of nothing.

"Yes," I replied, liking the sound of that phrase.

"I've been commissioned by a publisher to produce a series of business books," he went on. "I'd like to do them because it's good for business, but I don't have the time. Why don't you write them for me? I'll get the glory and you can have the money."

I was insulted for about five seconds and then I saw the potential of what he was offering. The books already had a publisher. It was definite money. All the information was in one place and would be relatively easy to collect. He was an interesting man with a lot to teach me. When I reflected a little further I realised that I had actually been doing much the same thing in journalistic form for clients of public relations companies, writing articles and speeches on their behalf. This was merely a protracted version of the same process.

I accepted the job and it went without a hitch. There must, I thought once it was over, be millions of people with books in their heads who don't have the time, ability or inclination to write them themselves. I just need to find them. That was when I hit upon the idea of taking a small ad in *The Bookseller* — "Ghostwriter for Hire" — in the hope of reaching every publisher and literary agent who had a client with a great story but no time or inclination to write it themselves.

The story of Stumpy

My ghostwriting gene must have developed early. I didn't realise that what I was doing was going to be my life's career but at the age of around 11 I decided, with the help of my best friend, Tom, to write the life story of Stumpy.

Stumpy was one of many mice that I had bred in the school nature society (a society of which I was voted President, I'll have you know, largely because my mice bred with greater speed and ferocity than anyone else's), but he was different, born with only three functioning legs. I guess this could be described as my first "misery memoir".

Every bit of free time we could squeeze from the dreary daily routine of boarding school, Tom and I would hurry off down the corridors to the school library — a permanently unpopulated, panelled room with floor to ceiling shelves of unread books, looking out over terraces to the valley beyond — to write another chapter of Stumpy's autobiography ... Even then I should probably have been taking more fresh air and physical exercise.

The glamour model versus the "arbiters of taste"

"I've had a call," the agent said, "from the managers of a model called Jordan. She's looking for a ghostwriter for an autobiography."

"Who?"

It was the beginning of the twenty-first century and unless you were a regular reader of *The Sun* newspaper, you did not necessarily know who Jordan was or what her story might be.

"She's famous for having had her breasts enlarged. Her management are asking publishers for a million pound advance. Do you think it would be worth meeting her?"

"She sounds like an interesting character."

The agent was Andrew Lownie, one of the most distinguished independents in the business. He was one of the agents who responded to my ad in *The Bookseller* and we had worked together very successfully on a number of projects, all very different to this one. He agreed to set up a meeting and rang back a few hours later.

"They want to have the meeting at her lawyer's offices: Mishcon de Reya."

"Mishcon de Reya! Seriously?"

This was one of the biggest-hitting law firms in London. They had acted for the Princess of Wales in her divorce. This Jordan girl was not messing about. Lord alone knew how much a firm like this would be charging for their services.

The meeting room was surprisingly full when we arrived and I couldn't help wondering how many of the shiny male managers and lawyers around the shiny conference table were charging by the hour.

Jordan, in the sort of skimpy dress a "saucy French maid" might wear in a farce, had brought a friend with her and seemed totally relaxed in the surroundings despite the fact that she can't have been much more than 25 years old. The two of them chatted and giggled like they were in Starbucks while the men attempted to talk business. Every so often, however, Jordan would interject with a question which completely cut through all the bullshit, and hold the eyes of whomever she was talking to with a disarming — and slightly alarming — intensity. I wasn't completely convinced that she had enough of a story for a whole book, but I was completely convinced she would be fun to work with. She too said she would be interested.

After the meeting I made a few phone calls around publishers and other agents that I knew, just casually asking if they had heard of Jordan and whether they thought there was anything in it. With each phone call I found out more. It seemed that Jordan's management team had already been to virtually every agent and publisher in the business, leading the conversation with the announcement that they were looking for a million pound advance.

I wasn't surprised that this request was being greeted with derision by the industry but what did shock me was the level of disdain with which they all seemed to dismiss the would-be author herself, simply because of her profession and because of the audience to whom they thought she appealed. Publishers who would happily buy biographies of courtesans, actresses and prostitutes of the past, seeing them as colourful players in the pageant of history, did not like the idea of dealing with a living, breathing woman who promoted herself to the masses as a sex object. To be frank, they didn't want to let her across their thresholds, let alone into the hushed and rarefied environs of their editorial departments. According to John Carey in his excellent book, *The Intellectuals and the Masses*, Rudyard Kipling observed that "the masses must pass into history before they become suitable for intellectual contemplation". Snobbery, it seems, is a constant, if mutating, presence in the literary world.

For a few months everything went quiet and Andrew Lownie lost interest in the project. I believe Jordan changed her management company and someone within Mishcon de Reya reached out to Maggie Hanbury, another distinguished literary agent, who for a while was under the impression that she was being asked to represent a Middle Eastern country. Once that misunderstanding had been cleared up Jordan worked her steely charm again and the two women found that they understood one another. Sadly for me, Hanbury decided that Jordan would be more comfortable talking to a female ghost and I fell out of the picture. I remained, however, fascinated with what was to unfurl over the following years.

Even with her new literary ally, Jordan was still not able to win over the arbiters of taste within the big publishing houses. One independent publisher, a former tabloid editor called John Blake, however, understood what he was being offered and thought that, with the addition of plenty of pictures, it would be a deal worth doing. He offered her an advance of £10,000, a hundred times less than her representatives had originally been asking for. Showing a flash of the business sense that would soon make her a multimillionaire, Jordan instructed her agent to accept the offer.

Two things then happened, which changed everything. John Blake came up with the idea of writing *Being Jordan* from the perspective of the real Katie Price, and Katie herself was invited to fly down to the Australian jungle and appear in *I'm a Celebrity . . . Get Me Out of Here*, where she caught the imagination of the British public, particularly the women, and conducted a very public romance with Peter Andre. A pop singer whose star had previously been waning, he became her first husband and father to two of her children. The target audience was no longer limited to male readers of *The Sun* because millions of women were now intrigued and wanted to know more and, as everyone in publishing knows, women are the ones who buy the most books, by a very large margin.

Being Jordan reputedly sold a million copies in hardback and editors in one of the major publishing houses who had previously refused to allow Jordan through their doors, were forced to offer Katie Price a seven figure sum to come to them with Rebecca Farnworth, her chosen ghostwriter. Cross with John Blake for signing up a rival model and for refusing to match this offer, Katie changed publishers and produced a stream of books in a variety of genres, most of which became colossal bestsellers, making no secret of the fact that she did not "do her own typing". At the time of writing this she and Rebecca are still a team, with Lord knows how many titles under their belts.

Secrets and confidentiality agreements

The ever-cheerful soap star peered suspiciously at the freshly delivered cover of her forthcoming autobiography.

"Why hasn't it got your name on it?" she enquired.

"Because I'm invisible," I reminded her. "It says so in my contract."

"Does it?" It was obviously the first she had heard of any such stipulation. "Why's that then?"

"The publisher thinks it's better."

"Why?"

"They think the fans will prefer to believe that you wrote it yourself. They want them to picture you sitting down at your escritoire at the end of a hard day's filming and pouring your heart out onto the page."

"Sitting at my what?"

"Your writing desk."

She emitted a tobacco-throated croak of mirth. "I don't think anyone's that thick, are they?"

"It's standard practice. The publisher just thinks it's better."

"I'm not sure about that. I don't want people to think that I'm pretending I can write a book. That'll make me look like a right knob."

Such frankness is always endearing in an author. Most, in my experience, are quite happy to confess that they have had help with "doing the typing", as Katie Price would say; it is usually the lawyers and the publishers who insist on contracts that threaten the ghost with hanging, drawing and quartering if they even tell their pet spaniel that their clients didn't write their own books. The paid advisers are equally fond of confidentiality agreements that forbid you from ever telling anyone anything that you might have found out that doesn't actually make it into the published book. If the client removes all their clothes during a recording session or confides that they intend to top themselves, mum's the word.

Things have become less draconian with the passing years and with the public's growing awareness that most people will find it hard to dash off a book if they are also doing another full-time job like starring in a soap opera, playing in a professional football team or running a country. As a result there are now some books where the ghost is openly acknowledged on the cover or the flyleaf and is free to talk to everyone including the media about their involvement in the project, and others where quite the opposite is true. Likewise there are some author/ghost relationships where a level of trust exists without the necessity of a written confidentiality contract, and a ghost would guard their author's secrets as fiercely as they would guard those of their friends and family. Those are the best ones. It is the state that all good ghosts should aspire to.

Glimpses of hell

Living, as I do, in one of the safest and most prosperous islands in the world, and being part of a comfortable and loving family, it is easy to forget or to remain ignorant of the depths of hellishness that man is capable of inflicting on his fellow man, and frequently does. The collapse of the communist Eastern Bloc at the end of the eighties released a hurricane of shocking and fascinating human interest stories, carried back to the West by people who needed the help of ghostwriters to tell them.

When Romanian President, Nicolae Ceauşescu, was toppled from power and executed in 1989 his country was released from a quarter of a century of oppression. What horrified the outside world the most, however, was what was discovered inside the walls of the "orphanages for the irrecuperable" which littered the country. Thousands of children who had been deemed to be of no use to Romania, or who had been "inconvenient" births, were found locked up in these asylums, tied up in cots, starved, abused, driven insane and beaten until they eventually gave up living. This was what medieval Bedlams must have looked like.

Western cameras went in and recorded scenes the like of which we had not seen in Europe since the liberation of the concentration camps after the Second World War.

After the collapse of Yugoslavia stories of war crimes and ethnic cleansing emerged daily as different factions and nationalities struggled to fill the power vacuum, committing any atrocities they deemed necessary. Soldiers, doctors, diplomats and charity workers all came out of the area with tales of unbelievable barbarity and many of them also needed ghostwriters to help them put into words horrors that had left them speechless.

The symbolic fall of the Berlin Wall seemed like a new beginning. Although the stories that had been hiding behind it were more prosaic than we had been led to believe by the propaganda of the Cold War, at a personal level they were both shocking and awe-inspiring. Individual stories of endless, grinding poverty, cruelty and darkness emerged into the light. Each story that was brought to me seemed more gruelling and shocking than the one before.

Out of that darkness, however, it was possible to make out glimmers of hope as good people made huge sacrifices and put their own lives on hold in order to help. A variety of ghostwritten books followed. There were tales of hopelessly crippled and apparently mad orphans being saved by Western surgeons and by the love of patient foster families. Bombed orphanages were rebuilt by soldiers, charities were set up and families who had been separated for a generation were reunited. There was so much to do but no shortage of people who wanted to help, and who then wanted to tell the stories of the horrors and the miracles they had witnessed.

For a writer it was a Pandora's box: scenes of unspeakable evil and personal struggles, often leading to happy endings. I wrote the story of a small boy who had been tied up and imprisoned in an orphanage cot for the first four years of his life, condemned by the authorities as sub-human because he was believed to be both physically and mentally handicapped, who was saved by a volunteer and given a full life in the West. I did one for a soldier who rebuilt a bombed orphanage for a local town in his own time and went on to create a full-scale charity, and another for an English woman who had been trapped in Eastern Europe as a teenager just before the Second World War, not escaping back to her family in the West until the Iron Curtain finally fell just over half a century later. I also helped tell tales for some of the pioneering business pirates and ex-politicians who built vast fortunes as communism crumbled and a new frontier-land of opportunities opened up for those bold and ruthless enough to grab them.

These stories were the absolute stuff of life, horrifying and inspiring, sickening and uplifting, frightening and dramatic. I seldom cried while I was actually there in the orphanages, or actually listening to the stories (as Graham Greene once said "There is a splinter of ice in the heart of a writer"), but I confess that when I came to write the stories the ice would inevitably melt into tears. The goal then was to ensure that the readers would be equally moved to tears at the same time as being unable to stop turning the pages.

That splinter of ice

That "splinter of ice in the heart of a writer" Greene talked about helps a great deal when listening to stories that have the potential to break your heart. Ghosts, like other authors, need to be able to remain objective, slightly distant, hovering above the emotion, watching and noting what it looks and sounds like. But at the same time we need to understand what it feels like in order to convey it to the reader.

If the person who is telling you the story is crying, then you need to be able to make the reader cry too when you reproduce the story on the page, but you won't be able to do that if you get too close. You need to be interested in the story, amazed by it, moved by it, but you cannot let it cloud the clarity of your own thoughts while you are interviewing.

Sometimes I have sat with people who are in floods of tears when they tell their stories. More often they struggle to hold in those tears, their chins trembling, their eyes and noses running involuntarily, their voices cracking as they battle bravely on with the memories that cause them so much pain and which they want so much to exorcise. It is a cliché that many of the soldiers who had the most traumatic times in the trenches of the First World War never wanted to speak about their experiences once they got home. The same rule has applied to others who have suffered since in different ways but times have changed. The medical profession came to understand about post-traumatic stress and people are now encouraged to talk about their traumas in order to learn how to cope with them. It is still never an easy thing for most damaged people to do.

My role is to sit and wait, quiet and encouraging; never criticising them, never comforting them, never rushing them, just passing the tissues, assuring them there is no problem and waiting for them to feel able to continue.

Readers want to be moved to tears by stories, just as they want to be moved to laughter or to shrieks of fear. They want to "feel something". A ghostwriter must catch the elements that produce that effect and reproduce them later on the page, not during the interview.

I guess therapists and analysts must work in the same way because often when I get to the end of the interviewing process the subject will say they feel like they have just been through a course of therapy. They are nearly always grateful to have been able to unburden themselves but still the fact remains that there was a splinter of ice required in order to achieve it — and that troubles me a little.

It isn't only once work is under way that a ghost has to remain detached. Often the people who make initial enquiries about hiring a ghostwriter have heartbreaking tales to tell. To have to warn them that the fact that they have lost a child in appalling circumstances or been tortured for months by an oppressive regime does not necessarily mean that they will get a publishing deal, can seem unbearably cruel — but to give them false hope would be far crueller.

I suppose it's the same in many other professions. A paediatrician must spend a large proportion of his or her time having to give heartbreaking news to parents. A press photographer sent to a war or disaster zone, a policeman dealing with the victims of a terrible crime or having to break the news of a death to a family. All these people can only function effectively in their jobs if they become detached in some way, deliberately inserting Greene's cold, hard, necessary splinter of ice.

Suddenly you're history

Since these are my confessions, I guess I must reveal that I was more than a little in love with Twiggy when I was a schoolboy in the sixties. Although she was about four years older than me she did not seem as intimidatingly mature and grown up as the other models and film stars that my generation of boys were busily lusting after. In fact, she didn't look that different to some of us when we were made-up to appear on stage in school plays. It was quite possible to imagine yourself on a date with her, despite her extraordinary and unusual beauty — not to mention her enormous global fame and iconic status.

So, when a publisher rang in the mid-nineties and asked if I would come to the office for lunch with Twiggy as she was looking for a ghostwriter, it set all my nostalgia glands tingling.

The lunch was delightful. Twiggy was delightful, and even though I didn't get the job (again I was told they had decided a woman would be more suitable), I felt I had an anecdote that might at least interest, and possibly even impress, my children.

"I had lunch with Twiggy last week," I announced casually over Sunday lunch.

"Twiggy?" my eldest daughter exclaimed, looking just as stunned as I thought appropriate for such a momentous event. "That's amazing. We're doing her at school, in history."

Abused children find a voice

At the beginning of the nineties I started to receive phone calls and letters from people who wanted to write about abuses they had suffered in their childhoods. These were not people who had had the misfortune to be born in countries that were enduring brutal dictatorships, civil wars or ethnic cleansing campaigns, these were people who had been born and brought up in democratic, peacetime Britain, a country that prided itself on being civilised, with developed social welfare services.

Their calls seemed to be cries for help and as I talked to them I became aware of just how much courage it had taken most of them to pick up the phone in the first place. These were people whose experiences did not lead them to expect to be listened to or believed but they had the courage to keep on trying to tell their stories. Many of the things they told me tore my heart out and I felt sure there would be a readership for them if I could just get them out into the bookshops.

I wanted to find out more about their lives and I wanted to help them to tell their stories as movingly and dramatically as possible. It seemed likely that if these stories were moving me then they would move other people as well.

When, as a teenager, I read *Down and Out in Paris and London* by George Orwell I had been particularly struck by a scene in Paris where Orwell reports meeting a man called Charlie, whom he describes as "a local curiosity". Charlie tells of visiting a girl who is being kept prisoner in a cellar which had been tricked out as a bordello-style bedroom and was guarded upstairs by an old crone. Charlie told how he gave the old woman a thousand francs, which he had stolen from his drunken brother.

"*Voilà*," the woman said, "go down into the cellar there and do what you like. I shall see nothing, hear nothing, know nothing. You are free, you understand — perfectly free."

Orwell reports Charlie's experiences in the cellar as if they make Charlie an interesting and colourful character, but it struck me that it was the girl whose story was actually the most mysterious and interesting. How had she got there? Who had betrayed her? What was the rest of her life like? What was she thinking? What were her dreams? What became of her? Her story seemed more intriguing than the story of the narrator (Orwell himself), an Old Etonian playing at being a "*plongeur*" for a while (a bit like an early version of the student gap year), before becoming a literary legend.

The stories that I was now hearing seemed just as fascinating, coming from a dark world that was unknown to me and that I wanted to understand better. I couldn't understand how so many people could be getting away with abusing children and I had difficulty imagining what it must feel like to be one of those children. It seemed to me that it would be a good thing to shine some bright lights into these dark corners of the human experience, so that everyone could understand more. They also seemed to me to be perfect fairy tales; good versus evil, innocent little heroes and heroines fighting back against terrible villains.

Filled with optimism I kept listening to the stories, writing synopses and sample material and trying to persuade publishers that they should publish them. The reaction was always the same: "No one," the publishers all informed me, "wants to read such gruelling and depressing stories." Child abuse, they believed, was all too horrible to contemplate. Even amongst the most liberal of them I could detect scepticism; was it possible that such terrible things could be happening in our own country? Surely not.

But what, I kept asking, were pantomimes like *Cinderella* and *Snow White* about if it wasn't child abuse? And what about Dickens's tales from the workhouses and back streets of Victorian England? Do we really believe that the Artful Dodger and his pals were required to do nothing worse than steal a few pocket handkerchiefs and watches on behalf of their violent, thieving, drunken masters? Even the orphaned Harry Potter starts out abused by the aunt and uncle charged with his guardianship.

I truly couldn't understand how the same publisher could produce so many books about war, genocide and murder, creating bestsellers by glamorising, stylising and fetishising serial killers and rapists, mafia bosses and military leaders, and at the same time think that genuine, original stories by children who had been victimised were somehow too tasteless to be told.

Then in 1993 Dave Pelzer self-published his memoir, *A Child Called It*, in America, and it became a word-of-mouth bestseller, filtering up into my consciousness via my children and their friends, who were passing it around in the school playground, much to the consternation of some of their parents and teachers.

A few years later I received an email from a man who wanted to write something similar about his own childhood with a violent and abusive mother. I warned him that my experience told me I might not be able to sell the book to publishers. He said that he was willing to take the risk and wanted to commission me to write the book anyway.

It was a good story. Once it was completed I sent it to Barbara Levy, an exceptionally discreet and gentle agent, who I knew would be sympathetic when it came time to break the bad news to the author that it was unsaleable. I had reckoned without the "Pelzer-factor".

Within a week Barbara had three publishers making offers and the book went for a six figure advance. It then sat at the top of the bestseller lists for weeks and eventually went on to be made into a movie. The game had changed entirely. Other publishers saw this success and remembered that I had been in to see them in the past. They started ringing to find out if I still had any other stories that could be packaged in a similar way. On one memorable day editors from three different publishing houses, all having just come from editorial planning meetings, rang within a few hours of one another with the same request. I had plenty of stories ready and waiting, all I had to do was introduce the people with the stories to the people who now really wanted the stories, and then write them.

The demand seemed insatiable. Supermarkets started to stock the resulting titles in massive quantities and kept asking the publishers for more. I was in a publisher's office introducing one of these clients when another publisher, whom we had been to see earlier in the day, rang my mobile. I excused myself and slipped out of the room to take the call.

"If you leave that building now," the other publisher said, "I will give you quarter of a million pounds."

I felt like Tom Cruise in *Jerry Maguire*. The client and I then spent a surreal afternoon taking calls from the two publishers, finally clinching the deal before putting her back on her train home. Three months later exactly the same thing happened with another client's story of abuse. (I will be explaining later in the "filthy lucre" chapter how sums like this will soon be whittled away by reality to become far less dramatic figures, but these occasional episodes of apparent largesse on the part of publishers do at least provide temporary doses of adrenaline and optimism to any writer's life.)

Books that I wouldn't have been able to interest anyone in a few months before were now the objects of ferocious bidding wars between the publishers with the biggest cheque books. I ended up writing about a dozen of them, selling some in conjunction with agents such as Barbara Levy and Judith Chilcote and some under my own steam. For a while they virtually all became bestsellers. There was one week when there were actually three of them in the *Sunday Times* charts at the same time. In some cases I was contracted to remain anonymous, but several of them graciously put my name on the flyleaf, such as *The Little Prisoner* by Jane Elliott, *Just a Boy* by Richard McCann, *Daddy's Little Earner* by Maria Landon, *Cry Silent Tears* by Joe Peters and *Please, Daddy, No* by Stuart Howarth.

So, who was reading these books that the publishers had been so sure would be too terrible for anyone to bear? Initially there was the "tourist trade"; people who, like me, could not imagine what it must be like to live in such a world and wanted to understand it better. Then there were the actual citizens of this "hidden" world; the children who had suffered or witnessed abuse and were wanting the comfort of knowing that they were not alone. There is no way of ever quantifying how many people suffer some sort of bullying or abuse in their childhood which leaves them scarred in some way, but let's take a guess that it is around 10 per cent of the population. That includes those abused in the home, in care, or by authority figures like priests or school teachers. That is 6 million people in the UK alone.

Then there are those who simply want to read scary, tear-jerking tales about little heroes and heroines overcoming monsters; the same people who want to see Cinderella go to the ball and Oliver Twist escape from the clutches of Fagin and Bill Sykes.

People who had been keeping their own stories of abuse secret due to a mixture of fear and shame, suddenly saw that it was all right to speak out. The stories I was being brought grew more and more extreme and horrific. No one was going to be able to pretend that child abuse was not a problem in society any longer. The misery memoir phenomenon became a bubble, with all the big publishers rushing onto the shelves with look-alike products. Within a few years the market was saturated and books that would previously have been given advances of hundreds of thousands of pounds were having trouble finding publishers once more.

The genie, however, was now out of the bottle and it wasn't long before abusers and bullies were being named and shamed in any number of previously inviolable institutions from schools to churches, orphanages to mental hospitals and even the BBC, to a point where it started to look to some like a witch hunt.

Some time later I heard a highly distinguished publisher on a podium being asked by a member of the audience what he thought of the "misery memoir" genre. He was not one of those who had joined in the gold rush and I assumed that he was going to say something dismissive.

"I think they changed the art of autobiography for ever," he said. "They forced authors to be much more open and revelatory. It is no longer good enough to tell anecdotes about the day you 'met Prince Philip' or 'danced with Sammy Davis Junior'; if you want to capture the hearts of readers you have to open up your emotional life as well and talk honestly and from the heart. I think they did the genre a great service."

Sacked by a glove puppet

Everyone around the boardroom table was entirely in agreement; at no stage and no time was anyone allowed to admit out loud or in writing that our celebrity was not a real person. Never mind that the celebrity in question was made of felt, this was the merchandising business, there had to be rules. The lawyers insisted.

My job, as the chosen ghostwriter, was to produce an autobiography which would fill in this celebrity's back story, his early life before he found fame, and exactly what happened to him in the "wilderness years" before his comeback as a potentially money-making merchandising vehicle. There were many careers resting on the outcome of this exercise, most of them sitting round that table in their shirtsleeves — brainstorming and sipping mineral water.

I had been hired by the distinguished publisher who had agreed to bring the eventual book out under his distinguished imprint. It was a nice job for both of us. For me it felt a bit like being given a licence to write fiction (although, of course, it wasn't fiction because the lawyers said so and the story must, therefore, be spoken of at all times as non-fiction, even though I was going to be making it up).

One of the golden rules of writing both fiction and non-fiction must be to be fundamentally truthful in your writing, and if you aren't going to be truthful then you'd better be as entertaining as hell. But, of course, truthful was the option to go for here, because the lawyers said so.

Our hero had found fame in the seventies and we all know how badly celebrities were allowed to behave in those days. Now, it seemed to me, was the time for him to 'fess up to every little indiscretion (this was before the really heinous and unamusing revelations of the period started to emerge). I was also sure readers would understand exactly why he went off the rails during the wilderness years — wouldn't everyone if subjected to the pressures of sudden fame and fortune? To hold on to the readers' sympathies I felt we must come clean about the addictions and the dodgy business deals that he had become involved in during those years at the same time as dropping the names of all the celebrities he had mingled with.

Once the manuscript was finished and both the distinguished publisher and I were happy that we had done full justice to the whole Greek tragedy of this celebrity's rise and fall and resurrection, there was another meeting in the same boardroom. We arrived, feeling extremely pleased with ourselves, but now the men and women in shirtsleeves were no longer smiling. The celebrity, apparently, was not happy with the way he had come across. The ghost was going to have to be replaced by someone who understood what was expected of them.

"The thing we have to remember," the distinguished publisher sighed as we stood on the street outside, forlornly scouring the horizon for a taxi to whisk us away from the scene of our humiliation, "is that nobody around that table has ever commissioned anything bigger than a fridge magnet."

I felt better for his wise words.

A debt to Dale Carnegie

"You're like a human Hoover," my wife complained as we drove home from the dinner party. "That poor woman . . ."

"What poor woman?" I truly didn't know what she was talking about. I had been basking in the afterglow of what I thought had been a pleasant evening out.

"The one you were cross-examining about her love life."

"I wasn't cross-examining her," I protested, "I just pressed the button and everything poured out. She was a human Nespresso machine."

"You do it all the time. You're like the Spanish Inquisition. Some people like to preserve a little privacy, you know."

She was right, of course, I do it all the time, but in my experience most people love talking about themselves, and those who don't pretty quickly clam up or tell me to mind my own business. It was a secret I learned at the age of 17 when I was heading for London in search of streets paved with gold with virtually no social skills at all.

How, I wondered as I watched those around me socialising with apparent ease, did people find things to talk about to strangers at parties? How did you find things to say to young women on first dates? (Bearing in mind that my early romantic education had come from the regency novels of my mother's Georgette Heyer collection, since when I had been incarcerated in single-sex boarding schools.) The adult world seemed a daunting, if exciting, place and I was desperate to discover the secret of all the grown-ups who seemed so self-confident in every social situation.

In my search for a magic formula I came across *How to Win Friends and Influence People* by Dale Carnegie. The book had been written in 1936, so was already more than 30 years old and more than 40 years later I can still remember the key message. Mr Carnegie explained that virtually everyone loves to talk about themselves and about their pet subjects. If you keep asking them questions they will keep answering them and the more they talk the more material you have for follow-up questions. The vast majority of people will come away from the conversation thinking you are the most charming and interesting person in the world, even if they have not asked you a single question about yourself (and it is my experience that a shocking number of people will fall silent the moment you stop asking the questions, even at private dinner tables where you would assume they wanted to be polite).

For a self-conscious teenager setting out to enter the adult world this one piece of advice was priceless; for someone wanting to make a living as an author and ghostwriter it has proved invaluable.

Over the years it has become such an ingrained habit that there is more than a little truth in my wife's fear that the technique can be intimidating for those who might be unused to talking about themselves. Of course, it should be applied with some sensitivity, but at the same time there are so many questions which are so fascinating they are irresistible, even if they are considered impertinent: how much do you earn? Why did you divorce your husband? Are you having an affair with that man over there? Why do you suppose your children hate you? . . . It's amazing how many people reward straight questions with extremely full and revealing answers.

The first questions a ghostwriter should ask

The first questions you ask in any relationship are always the hardest. The answers you receive are going to become the signposts for the journey the conversation is going to take from then on.

I receive three or four enquiries a day from people who want to write books, mostly via email in recent years. The first things I ask for are a brief synopsis of the story (the sort of thing we might eventually see on the back cover), and some explanation of what their expectations are for the book. Are they hoping for a bestseller, for instance, or do they want to self-publish a few copies for friends and family?

Most are able to respond to those questions, however unsure they may be of their own ability with words. If they find writing even that much is beyond them then we might try opening the dialogue in a phone call.

Once I start the actual process of listening to the story it is always a good idea to begin at the beginning and work forward chronologically, even if the early days of someone's life appear irrelevant to the story they actually want to tell. The ghost needs to get to know them in order to recognise what questions to ask later. Only by knowing what has gone before will the ghost be able to gauge how they will think, feel and react in certain situations. Starting by talking about their earliest memories and perhaps their relationship with their parents, is nearly always going to break the ice nicely. Once the ice is broken and they feel comfortable the conversation will flow quite normally, with the ghost simply steering the chronology like a sheepdog herding memories instead of sheep, ferreting out the details as and when they are required in order to be able to visualise and understand the stories that are being told.

In many ways a ghostwriter is merely asking all the same questions that a reader would ask if they were in the room with the author rather than reading the eventual book.

"You need to come to Haiti..."

I have to confess that there have been many times when I have accepted an invitation to a destination simply because I have read and loved a book about the place (*The World of Suzie Wong* for Hong Kong, *Breakfast at Tiffany's* for New York, *Death in Venice* for Venice, *Myra Breckinridge* for Hollywood, *Don't Stop the Carnival* for the Caribbean islands generally, *The Great Railway Bazaar* for the art of travel itself, and so forth).

I must have read Graham Greene's *The Comedians* pretty soon after it was published in 1966, when I would still have been in my teens (I had probably seen the film too, which was produced as a vehicle for Elizabeth Taylor and Richard Burton the following year).

Greene had already caught my attention with both his stories and his own life, taking my imagination to some of the darkest and most frightening places on earth. *The Comedians* painted a picture of Haiti under the tyrannical "Papa Doc", who used the fearful power of Voodoo and his private army, the Tonton Macoutes, to control the people. It seemed like the most exotic and dangerous place a man could ever hope to travel to

48

and Greene's story was filled with the sort of damaged characters who roam to such places in search of quick fortunes and adventure, always living on the outside.

In the early eighties I was hawking my services as a travel writer to anyone in a position to dole out a free flight or a bit of board and lodging. I had been spending time on a number of Caribbean islands like Jamaica, St Lucia and Barbados, where it was not hard to find tourist authorities and hotel owners who were willing to entertain a freelance writer for a while in exchange for articles about their islands and their facilities. Haiti, however, was going to be a harder nut to crack and I lacked the nerve to simply turn up at Port-au-Prince and take my chances.

By that time Papa Doc's son, "Baby Doc", who was only a couple of years older than me, was President and the darkness of tyranny that Greene had depicted so chillingly had, if anything, deepened. The only news stories that came out of the island were bad ones, making it all the more intriguing. I had written to the island's consulate, making preliminary enquiries but not holding out much hope of a reply, when I received a phone call from a British businessman who had made his home in Haiti and was extremely keen to promote the place.

"You need to come to Haiti," he told me, "everyone has opinions about it but no one really knows it. You can stay with us and I'll show you the real island."

It was an invitation I was definitely not going to turn down. It was a chance to experience first-hand how an ex-pat lived in such a place, and I would have someone to guide me in Greene's footsteps. Perfect.

Baby Doc would be ensconced in the white folly of a presidential palace for only a few more years before he was overthrown and fled into exile on the French Riviera. The palace now lies in ruins, as uninhabitable as the rest of the city around it, but then it still gleamed like a heavily guarded wedding cake amidst the squalor as I stood outside the gates staring in, trying to imagine the domestic life of the tyrant and his family, wondering how they managed to justify their actions to themselves and to one another. It was a curiosity which would later tempt me to accept invitations to the palaces of other tyrants, wanting to see what made them different, wanting to understand how they had found themselves in such extreme situations, able to exert their terrible will over whole populations.

The exotic Grand Hotel Oloffson, where Greene had set most of his story (calling it the Hotel Trianon), still stood on the outskirts of Port-au-Prince and one of Greene's original characters, Aubelin Jolicoeur (the gossip columnist, Petit Pierre, in the book), still propped up the bar.

"He has made himself one of the country's leading characters," I wrote at the time, "affecting cane, monocle, cravat and a theatrically camp manner which makes many unaware of just how much influence he has at the presidential palace and in ministerial offices."

In one of those ministerial offices I met the island's then director of tourism, "a Gucci-clad minister by the name of Theo Duval".

"Why do we travel?" he mused. "To feel in a pleasant way, to make a loop in the straight line of our existence, escaping into timelessness, a dreamlike state in which we are not reminded of our servitude."

It was the first truly poor place I had ever visited and I was shocked to see how close to the brink of chaos people can survive, and frightened to see how fragile a veneer civilisation actually is.

The Comedians ends with one of the departing characters throwing a handful of coins from a car window, causing a dangerous riot amongst the scrabbling horde of street children — an image which we would later see magnified and repeated nightly on the news after the island was repeatedly hit by natural disasters.

"When people come to Haiti," Aubelin Jolicoeur told me in the hotel bar as the tropical night-rains crashed down on the roof of the veranda outside, "they always try to make the story funny. They never take it seriously. All through the centuries we have been ostracised by the world because we were the first black republic. Always we are misunderstood and misinterpreted. There is a bad spell on Haiti."

Tyrants and other
interesting monsters

I have to confess that the first (and sometimes only) criterion that I apply when deciding whether I want to do a book is whether I find the author and the story "interesting". The most "interesting" people, however, are not always the ones you would trust to care for your children, your grandmother or even your favourite puppy.

The people who are interesting are the ones who, at the time you come across them, inhabit a world you know nothing about and who know things that you want to find out. Sometimes those things can dwell on the darker, more secretive side of life.

Even before I tipped into my teenage years and became entranced by dark and complex characters like Lord Byron and the occultist, Aleister Crowley, I was intrigued by the horrific and indefensible. On a holiday to Spain with my parents I read Ernest Hemingway and became obsessed for a while with the glamour and horror of bullfighting and the matadors who seemed to me as dashing as real-life Scarlet Pimpernels. I nagged my parents into taking me to see El Cordobés (who was to bullfighting at the time what Elvis Presley was to popular music) and others fighting, and collected their autographs afterwards as if they were rock stars.

Before that Russell Thorndike's series of books following the adventures of Dr Syn (alias "The Scarecrow") made being a smuggler on the Romney Marshes seem like the most romantic pastime possible. Before that I dare say I formed my strong attachment to the sharp tang of marmalade thanks to the influence of Paddington Bear, who seemed to me more interesting and complex than Pooh Bear, who lusted after honey and lived close to where I was born. The familiar scenery of Ashdown Forest in Sussex could not compete in my imagination with Paddington's mysterious past in "Darkest Peru".

These days I guess it might be Grand Theft Auto or internet porn that first introduces impressionable young boys to the other side of good.

To me, "interesting" still means people the like of which I have not come across before, or people who have lived lives that I do not yet know anything about.

Had a charismatic young German leader contacted me in the twenties and asked me to help with a book he was planning, tentatively entitled *Mein Kampf*, I might well have skipped over as naively as a Mitford sister to see what the fuss was all about. Lord knows how long it would have been before the penny dropped and I realised the full horror of what this strange little man was actually talking about and I would then have ended up as deep in the soup as the unfortunate

P. G. Wodehouse. I might have been equally tempted by a ticket to China to volunteer to help Chairman Mao knock his thoughts into shape for the infamous *Little Red Book*.

Extremes of evil are as interesting as extremes of goodness. Extremes of wealth are as interesting as extremes of poverty. Without the bad guys there would be virtually no drama and no storylines strong enough to hold anyone's attention, no vampires or zombies or serial killers. Life is indeed a bitch.

Lunching with Imelda Marcos

Imelda Marcos was the wife of Ferdinand Marcos, the President of the Philippines, but she had a vacuous glamour all of her own, which was shored up by a glossy public relations machine designed to distract attention from the fact that she and her husband were allegedly fleecing their already poor country of record-breaking sums of money.

She arrived for lunch at one of Manila's showiest restaurants in a swirl of media attention, immaculately groomed and empty behind the eyes. Just the fact that she was taking lunch in public would be enough to ensure that all the local news programmes would carry the story. One of the many titles she had been awarded by her husband was Governor of Metropolitan Manila (along with Minister of Human Settlement, and Ambassador Plenipotentiary and Extraordinary). Her husband's health was known to be failing and it was said that she was effectively the acting President. There was also speculation at that time that if he were to die, she and her husband's trusted military adviser would seize power together.

The organisers of the lunch, and indeed of the whole trip, had been a little vague about what they hoped would come from this meeting. Their brief seemed to be to promote the Philippines as a destination and the first couple as glorious, benevolent rulers.

During the lunch, with every spoonful of food being filmed for the edification of the hungry viewing public, she said absolutely nothing of any interest whatsoever and it was entirely unclear whether anyone had actually managed to make her understand that they were thinking of asking her to write a book. Her face was as devoid of expression as it was of wrinkles or blemishes. It was like sitting opposite a lovingly carved and polished religious icon, reverentially draped in designer clothes.

The Marcos family were overthrown a few years later and although it was found that they had stolen many billions of dollars from the people it was the discovery of Imelda's collection of 2,700 pairs of shoes which stuck most vividly in people's minds, an almost comic illustration of the superficiality of those who seek power and wealth for its own sake.

Afternoon tea with Mrs Mubarak

The man from the embassy insisted that it would be worth my while coming to London to meet his Minister of Information. He wouldn't tell me which embassy he was from or why this minister wanted to talk to me, but he managed to make me curious to find out more. The Minister was going to be staying at the Grosvenor House, one of the biggest and grandest hotels in Park Lane. I was scheduled to join him in the lounge for morning coffee.

The Minister and his officials were holding court around a large coffee table in front of a flaming log fire. His children, who were also staying as part of the entourage, drifted back and forth behind the sofas with family messages from the rooms upstairs as he cautiously revealed details of his mission. He had two books that he wanted written: the autobiography of President Hosni Mubarak and the autobiography of Mrs Mubarak, who had been at the President's side throughout his years in power as well as his time before that as Egypt's Air Chief Marshal and then Vice President.

I had a number of projects on the go at the time and didn't think that I would have the capacity to take on the President's life story with all the political sensitivities and complications that would be bound to bog everything down. I was also pretty sure that he and I would find it hard to form a good working relationship. I didn't know all that much about him personally at that stage but I knew enough about military rulers in general to be able to guess that we would not have much in common. I did think, however, that Mrs Mubarak's view on life in power would be interesting. She was half Welsh and half Egyptian, her parents having met while her father was a medical student in Wales, where her mother was a nurse. She had been with her husband on the podium in 1981 when President Sadat was assassinated beside them, at which moment she was catapulted into the role of First Lady of Egypt.

Suddenly everything was a rush and I was instructed to be on the next flight to Cairo. I'd never been to Egypt, even though it was the scene of my parents' first meeting during the Second World War. I owe my very existence to the hostess of a dinner party in Alexandria who decided to seat the young infantry Captain and the Wren (as members of the Women's Royal Naval Service were known) next to one another that evening.

"I don't have a visa," I warned the embassy official.

"Don't worry," I was assured by my new friend, "everything will be taken care of when you arrive."

Upon touchdown men in dark glasses and ear-pieces met me off the plane and I was whisked through separate channels at the airport and into a waiting Mercedes, which forced its way at speed through the clogged streets of the city, its siren wailing threateningly.

"Don't be scared," the man in the front passenger street grinned, "he is a highly trained police driver."

"I expect they said the same thing to Princess Diana and Dodi Fayed that night in Paris," my wife said when I rang her later.

The driver certainly was very skilful and all through the ride I was uncomfortably aware of the glowering resentment emanating from the pedestrians forced to jump out of our way and the cars forced to pull over. It seemed like I had accidentally allowed myself to be recruited to the bullies' gang in this hot, angry, overcrowded urban playground.

The hotel I had been put in was a fortress beside the Nile. Filled with cool air and wide open spaces it was a million miles from the heat and the crowds and the smells outside.

It was a couple of days before Mrs Mubarak was ready to receive me. More men with mobile phones and dark glasses arrived at the hotel in another limousine and as we drew closer to the palace the armed guards waved us through one layer of security after another, until we eventually arrived in a secluded courtyard outside a private front door, where a butler and the Minister of Information were waiting to usher me the final few yards.

The Minister seemed to have lost all the expansive self-confidence that he had shown when holding court at the Grosvenor House as he nervously briefed me on how I should behave in the presence of his First Lady.

Tea was laid out in an elegant salon, served by a team of waiters in white jackets and black bow ties. Mrs Mubarak arrived as if borne on a fragrant cloud of graciousness and made conversation with all the non-committal charm of a woman who has been socialising at diplomatic levels for all of her adult life, groomed in much the same immaculate international style as Imelda Marcos.

The scion of a South American dictator's family, who had reached the zenith of their powers in the sixties, was once trying to paint a picture for me of his mother and the other women in the family at that time. "They all wanted to look the same," he explained. "They all wanted to look like Jackie Kennedy." So many of our greatest visual historical references are created by the momentary whims of great fashion designers and hairdressers.

Inside Mrs Mubarak's gilded salon it was impossible to imagine that we were still in the same hot and angry city that I had been exploring for the previous two days. She didn't hesitate to give spontaneous answers to the stream of questions that I had, despite the fact that the Minister was squirming with discomfort next to me on the slippery silk of the sofa. There was so much that I wanted to know. It seemed like a story that a lot of women married to ambitious men might well be able to identify with, while at the same time giving a glimpse of what life was like behind palace walls for the edification of the billions who would always remain locked outside.

A few months later the green shoots of the Arab Spring started to break through and Mrs Mubarak and her husband would prove to be two of its most conspicuous casualties. From the palace he and their sons were put first under house arrest before being taken to a prison and then on to a courtroom. It was not at all certain that they would be allowed to live through the process. Eight months later neighbouring Libya's transparently evil and increasingly demented ruler, Gaddafi, was stabbed to death by his people, his sons and other followers also executed, the full horror of their crimes exposed to the world, followed by the full horror of what would come after their falls.

In Egypt accusations flew that the Mubarak family had salted tens of billions of dollars away in places like Switzerland and the UK and that the President had failed to stop the killing of peaceful protestors. Tales of torture and oppression billowed out from the inferno of accusations. The world hailed the Egyptian "revolution" as the most successful and democratic of processes. There was a general feeling of euphoria and hope that the whole area might be on the verge of new levels of personal freedom. Democratic elections followed but two years later there was a backlash. Terrible bloodshed erupted in Cairo once more and Hosni Mubarak was freed from jail with some talking of a return to power. It would have been interesting to have got to know the family better before their spectacular fall from grace.

Filthy lucre

It's vulgar to talk about money, I know, but it's so interesting to know how other people manage and to draw comparisons, which is invidious, but we've all got to earn the stuff somehow and if no one talks about it how do we ever learn what's going on?

The first criterion for considering any project is always whether I find it interesting enough to spend several months of my life thinking and writing about it. But there always has to be a second criterion too — can the project be made to pay in some way?

The moment you decide that you are going to earn your living as a freelance writer (or a freelance anything for that matter), you condemn yourself to a lifetime of thinking about money. Every day you will find yourself frantically doing sums in your head when you should be thinking about something more productive, trying to reconcile the money that you think you are going to be earning in the next month or two with the bills that you know for sure are going to be coming in.

You have only a limited number of hours in every day and so you cannot waste too many of them on speculative projects that don't work out. But at the same time you know that it is often the speculative projects, the biggest gambles, that produce the most dramatic results. But which ones? There is no way of knowing. Can you afford to do ten speculative books in the hope that one of them will prove to be a bestseller and compensate if the other nine fail to earn a bean? These are the questions that will be haunting you as you try to get to sleep at night, and will still be there when you wake up in the morning, and linger around in the background for most of the hours in between.

As you get older and take on family responsibilities the calculations grow more urgent and more hours of work have to be found at just the moment when other demands on your time are increasing. Sometimes you must choose projects with good commercial potential over those with more literary appeal. Sometimes you must tilt the telling of a story in ways that might not be to your personal taste in order to appeal to as wide a market as possible. You can blame the commercial demands of the publisher for such lapses if you like, but the truth is you stand to gain as much from increased sales and happier readers as they do.

Some writers escape from the financial treadmill when they hit upon an unexpected seam of gold (*Harry Potter, Fifty Shades*, etc.), others supplement their writing with earnings from broadcasting, journalism or university teaching. Yet more treat writing as a sideline, being primarily professors, chefs, actors or television presenters. If you do none of these things, concentrating on the writing of books as your sole source of income, you are going to have to grow ruthless in your self-discipline both in the projects that you agree to take on and in the hours that you work. It is a fabulous way to earn a living, but keeping the money coming in is grindingly and relentlessly distracting.

One of the sums that I used to use to try to cheer myself up on bad days was to extrapolate out possible future earnings by assuming they would continue to rise at the same level as in the past. Quite early on I had a particularly good year in which I managed to make twice as much as the year before. To avoid writing whatever it was I was meant to be writing, I immediately wasted my time drawing up a chart showing how much I would be earning in the future if I continued along the same line, doubling my income every year. By doing that you can go from £20,000 a year to over £20 million a year in just ten years.

I managed to remain quite excited by this prospect for some time, despite my wife's scepticism as to whether I had any grasp at all on the economic realities of life. The following year, however, I was back down at a figure somewhere between the previous two years and new graphs had to be thought up in order to remain optimistic.

The sums that publishers sometimes bandy around as advances can also be deceptive. If a publisher offers a quarter of a million pound advance it sounds like a lottery win, and feels like one for as long as it takes before you actually go away and do the sums. If the project is ghostwritten then that figure is going to be divided between two people and probably an agent will be taking 15 per cent as well. It will then be pointed out that the publisher wants two books for that money, so the money halves again and will be paid out in bits and pieces over the next two years, which comes out at £50,000 a year each for two years before tax. It's certainly a nice wage, but no longer looks quite so much like a lottery win. If the book then takes off there may well be royalties down the line, but more often than not the advance is the end of the story.

One of the benefits of having now been in the business for more than 40 years is that I can look back over the real figures and see that although it has been a bumpy ride, the overall line of the graph has risen pretty steadily, if slowly.

I now receive three or four enquiries a day from people thinking of hiring or working with a ghostwriter. Whereas at the beginning of my career I used to have to spend more than half my waking hours searching for such leads, I currently have the luxury of picking and choosing which opportunities I will pursue, mainly thanks to the internet and the magical powers of Google. In the past it was almost impossible for anyone outside the closed world of publishing to know where to start looking for a ghostwriter, now all they have to do is type the word into their search engine and hit the "enter" button.

Big Brother is watching and listening

"Why does it keep doing that?" my wife demanded when the bedside phone yet again let off a single ring just after we had fallen asleep, jolting us both back to wakefulness.

I had no sensible explanation to give her. I had tried explaining the problem to the phone company, but after coming out to check the physical line they were perplexed, only able to suggest that it was a fault with the handset. I'd tried replacing the handset but it had made no difference. The obvious answer would have been to take the phone out of the bedroom, but with elderly parents and young children who were starting to stay away quite frequently, that didn't seem like a helpful option.

"Rudi says it means they're bugging the phones," I said.

"Oh, for goodness' sake! Are you seriously suggesting that the government has time to listen in to all our conversations? You're becoming as paranoid as he is."

The logical part of my brain agreed with her, but on the other hand it did seem a bit of a coincidence that our phone had been behaving like this ever since I started having meetings with Rudi, a man who had just been let off a life sentence for spying for the Russians, having been caught and convicted at the height of the Cold War. By the time he was named by a KGB defector, Rudi had been active for 20 years and was probably the best placed agent the Russians had ever managed to recruit, with virtually unlimited access to information on projects like Exocet and Polaris. The country where he was caught was politically volatile and still practised the death penalty, so throughout the period of his imprisonment he had never been sure whether he would be executed or not. Changes in the political climate and in a number of regimes around the world, and an intervention from the Russian President, had led to him being pardoned and released after serving 10 years, at which point he went into hiding.

It was easy to imagine that the timing of these rings on our home phone fitted the picture he painted, as the eavesdroppers gave up listening for the night, assuming they would hear nothing interesting again until the morning.

If it was true they must have been disappointed because Rudi was adamant that we should never talk about anything over the phone, just as he always changed the venues for our meetings at the last minute to fox anyone who might be hoping to listen in. Interviewing him was never a restful business as his eyes darted around rooms, scrutinising everyone near us, noting when people came and went. If anyone got too close he would immediately stop talking and we would move on to a new venue. If we walked anywhere together he would take roundabout routes, often more than doubling the distance we needed to travel.

"Why would they still be interested?" I asked him one day. "The Cold War is over now."

He shook his head in despair at my naivety. "It's never over."

Revelations in 2013 about levels of surveillance from Edward Snowden, former CIA and NSA employee, suggest that Rudi might have been right.

The publishing world was not interested in Rudi's memoirs, believing that people had now moved on from the Cold War and were no longer excited by the idea of spies. Once we had abandoned the project our phone found itself able to rest peacefully once more.

It's always hard to know if you are being paranoid in these matters. Conspiracy theories are so tempting but can so easily be punctured with mockery. I was approached by a whistleblower who was in a position to cause considerable embarrassment to senior government officials. The man's name had become a byword for injustice in the media and was scrawled on motorway bridges at the time by supporters armed with aerosols. Publishers were keen to buy what he had to say.

A sturdy advance was negotiated by the agent involved and the day the first cheque arrived on the agent's desk the whistleblower was summoned in to talk to his government employers. They assured him they had no objection to him writing a book, in fact they thought it extremely "brave" of him, but they felt they did have to warn him that if he went ahead with publication they wouldn't be able to "guarantee his safety", or that of his family.

Since he had small children he had to take the warning seriously and we instructed the agent to return the money. He then asked me to return the diaries which he had given me to work from. Wanting to be sure that they arrived safely I went to the local village post office and asked the Postmistress to send them the most secure way possible. She advised sending them as registered documents.

Several days later the package had not arrived at its destination and I went back to the Postmistress and asked her to track it. She was happy to oblige, embarrassed to think that the service had let us down, but when she started to make enquiries she found that the parcel's trail ended abruptly at Gatwick Airport, never to be resumed.

But perhaps I am being paranoid again.

A real-life *Shades of Grey*

Their enquiry stood out from the others that came through that day. James emailed that he and his girlfriend, Penny, lived in Switzerland and were looking for a ghostwriter to tell their love story. He warned that it would contain sexual elements that many would find shocking, but that there would be many lessons to be learned from it.

> *Dear Mr Crofts, If possible, I think that meeting up with us, seeing who we are, hearing us out, would not be a waste of time.*

He told me they would be in London the following weekend and would be staying at the Dorchester in Park Lane. Curiosity got the better of me. *Fifty Shades of Grey* was selling millions of copies a week and female sexuality was the hot topic of the day. Since I was going to be in Mayfair anyway, interviewing an African leader whose memoir I was just finishing off, I suggested I pop into the Dorchester once I was finished.

The African leader had a busier schedule than expected and finding myself free in the middle of the day I sent James a text. He invited me to join them for lunch at Zuma, a famous Japanese restaurant in Knightsbridge. It seemed that fate was working to make this meeting both pleasant and convenient. Even if nothing came of the book it would be an interesting lunch and would pass the time until my African client was free once more.

The composed, confident couple I found waiting for me at the bar with perfectly chilled glasses of white wine were extremely good looking, but with no hint of arrogance. They managed to be both reserved and charming at the same time, intent on making me feel comfortable in their company despite the very obvious fact that they were completely wrapped up in their adoration of one another.

Plate after plate of tiny, elegant delicacies were presented at the table by discreet waitresses and one chilled bottle of wine followed another as they slowly revealed their fable of true love.

It started with love at first sight when they were little more than children and was shattered a few years later by the realities of adult life and the expectations of their families. Just like Romeo and Juliet the young lovers were forced apart by circumstances but, unlike Shakespeare's star-crossed lovers, these two had been given a second chance and they had turned it into something magical and extraordinary and deeply sexual.

By the time the espressos were being served I was hooked and had agreed to fly out to Switzerland the following weekend with a tape machine. That was the start of a journey deep into the lives of a couple who together have discovered some of the most profound secrets of personal happiness.

One of the skills necessary for ghostwriting is the ability to ask very personal questions without causing people to clam up with embarrassment. Exactly how far, I wondered, could I go with my questions this time? How much detail would they be willing to go into?

Initially Penny was more reserved in what she wanted to talk about than James was — although she didn't seem to think that she would be more comfortable with a female ghost, like Jordan and Twiggy — but gradually, as the three of us spent days together talking, she became more sure of what she wanted to reveal. Because James had done most of the talking initially the first draft of the book had too much of a male slant, but it made it possible for Penny to see what she didn't want and she started to open up more with her own descriptions of their relationship, both physical and emotional. That was when the book really started to take on a life of its own.

A gift for a billionaire

"Are you doing anything next weekend?"

I'd pulled the car over to take the call and was having trouble hearing my client's voice above the rushing traffic.

"No," I said, "I don't think so."

"It's my father's seventieth birthday and my mother's throwing him a party in Dubai. He's always saying one day he'll write a book and we thought we would give him a ghostwriter as a surprise birthday present."

"Jumping out of the cake you mean, like Marilyn Monroe in front of President Kennedy?" I joked.

"We can work out the details once you are there," he replied, obviously not ruling out the cake-jumping possibility. "I'll email you with the arrangements."

The email was already waiting in my inbox by the time I got home. My client was a wealthy businessman in his own right, based in London. His family was one of the richest and most powerful in Asia and his father was now the head of the large, extended dynasty. I guess it was a bit of a challenge to think what to give a man like that for his birthday. My flights were booked and a room was arranged in the seven-plus star hotel which had been totally commandeered by the family for the weekend. No one was to know why I was there until the presentation.

"What do I say if someone asks me who I am and why I'm at the party?" I asked when he phoned again to check everything was okay.

"Just say you're a friend of mine," he said, "no one will question it. And can you get a cover of the book mocked up to take with you, so we have something to show him?"

Photos of the great man arrived and I dashed off some copy for the back cover and inside flaps of the dust jacket, sending the package quickly to a friendly local publisher whose designers put the whole thing together in a remarkably convincing facsimile of a book that might actually exist. I headed for the airport a few days later.

There was a greeter from the organisers of the party waiting for me at the airport and she ferried me straight to the hotel where several hundred of the family's closest friends, relatives and business contacts were already ensconced. The entire hotel had been turned over to a carefully orchestrated private carnival. Guests had the run of the place and everything was provided at the expense of the hosts. I had always assumed that the parties depicted in *The Great Gatsby* were entirely imagined by F. Scott Fitzgerald, but I think he too must have been entertained in exactly this manner. Unless, of course, it was the other way round and modern billionaires are modelling their styles of entertaining on

Jay Gatsby's, even those who would never have read the original book.

I have to confess that it is a glorious feeling to be given permission to suspend your social conscience for a few days and allow yourself to be transported to a world where costs and prices are simply not a factor in anyone's plans. International stars are hired to entertain, banquets are spread out for guests to pick and choose from as and when they are troubled by the slightest pangs of hunger, and barmen constantly stand waiting to prepare whatever cocktail you ask for. All the guests had to worry about was what they would do next and what they should wear to do it. No doubt some of the seemingly social groupings of men in the various bars, restaurants and lounges were busily networking and setting up future deals, but most were simply there to catch up with people they hadn't seen since the last family gathering (which had involved a similar hotel arrangement in Penang a few months before), or meeting new people. The wives and children of the wealthy men passed the long hours playing cards or visiting the discreet jewellery shops that can always be found in such places.

There was indeed a cake, but thankfully it was constructed around a famous Asian supermodel and I was only required to stand demurely beside her as I was presented to the surprised, and initially puzzled, birthday boy.

Rich men's toys

"It's going to be hard to get quiet time together," the client said. "I've got a private jet and I go back and forth to New York a lot. That would be a good opportunity to talk without interruption."

"Sure," I agreed, always happy to meet a client wherever they would be most comfortable — particularly if it involved being pampered for a few hours in a private jet.

He was not the first wealthy client to make that suggestion and I doubted he would be the last. Some suggest taking a few days at spas, resorts or in country houses that they don't usually get much use from. Others like to do their talking on the decks and in the cabins of their yachts, even if we never travel more than a few miles off the Riviera coast and come ashore for dinner every evening.

Rich men love their toys and in most cases they also love to share them. If they are hiring a ghostwriter they already have an eye on how posterity will view them, and they want their scribe to see them at their best. On a commission in Hong Kong I couldn't understand why my client was being so cagey about inviting me to his house, always arranging our meetings in his office with its sweeping views out across the harbour. When the invitation finally arrived, on my last day in the city, his wife showed me their newly installed ornamental fish pond (a bit like the Trevi fountain in Rome only in white marble with gold decorations), and explained that her husband had not wanted me to see the house until the fountains and waterfalls were all working perfectly.

The mega-rich grow accustomed to perfection. Their days are kept peaceful and well oiled by immaculately discreet butlers, cooks and drivers. Their jets and limousines are more comfortably upholstered than most people's living rooms. They travel through life on a cloud of unruffled luxury and they see any interruption to that perfection as a failing. Many of them seem to be suffering from a variety of Obsessive Compulsive Disorder, which requires that they are cocooned at all times in a world of total order and cleanliness.

When I am getting to know them I try to get them to make all the decisions about where we should meet and what we should do together. Just as Nick Carraway entered the party-world of Jay Gatsby in order to tell his story and Charles Ryder became immersed in the aristocratic world of Brideshead, I want to sit in the rooms they use the most, eat what they eat, drink what they drink, go to the restaurants where they are known and comfortable. As Atticus Finch says in *To Kill a Mockingbird*: "You never really understand a person until you consider things from his point of view [. . .]

until you climb into his skin and walk around in it." Or in other words, "until you walk a mile in his shoes".

More than once a client has become impatient with my reluctance to express any preference as to where or what we should eat. They want to be generous and to supply whatever my needs might be — the Jay Gatsby syndrome again — when all I want is to get beneath their skins and see the world through their eyes and taste it through their food choices. If that means many hours trapped on private jets and yachts or in the luscious bowels of the Dorchester — so be it.

The soporific brothel

The idea came from the girl's husband, a British engineer who had been working for several years on a project in the Far East. He'd met her through mutual acquaintances. They fell instantly in love and married despite the fact that they didn't have a language in common. Over the following few years, as he taught her English, he learned the story of his young bride's life from the simple village where she was born to the brothels of Bangkok and eventually to freedom and security through marriage to him, a kind and gentle foreigner. He was proud of everything she had achieved and he thought that she deserved to have her story recognised, so on a business trip back to England he made contact with me.

"I would need to spend time with her," I explained, "would she come to London?"

"It would be better if you met her in Thailand," he said, "then you could see the actual places where the events happened."

Nobody paid any attention when the girl and I checked into the reception of the "hotel" in Bangkok where she had worked as a teenager. They were used to local girls and foreign men using the rooms upstairs.

One wall of the reception area was made of glass, behind which a selection of scantily clad girls and women sat or lay or wandered around, like bored specimens in an exotic aquarium. One of them was actually knitting as she waited. Every time a man moved towards the glass they would all burst into a frenzy of flirting and pouting, putting on performances that they hoped the shadowy figure behind the glass would find attractive, all wanting to be the one who was chosen to go upstairs, to be given a chance to earn an hour or two's wages.

Having paid the receptionist, my tiny guide and client led the way up to a small room furnished with nothing but a double bed and a bathtub. The ancient air-conditioning unit wedged in the window was stubbornly silent and the heat was overbearing.

"We can talk here," she said, climbing onto the bed, sitting cross-legged and opening her handbag. "You want a coke?"

Grateful for any sort of fluid I accepted the proffered bottle. When I unscrewed the lid a jet of warm sticky liquid sprayed out, soaking the already grubby sheets. She covered her mouth with dainty fingers, prettily smothering an involuntary giggle.

I took the tape machine from my pocket and laid it on the pillow.

"You sweating bad," she said, pointing to the dark patches on my T-shirt. "You take off shirt."

As I struggled out of the clinging T-shirt she took a swig from her bottle and lay down with her head beside the tape machine. I pressed the record button.

"Okay," I said, "let's start from the beginning."

I stretched out and propped my head up with my arm, so that I could watch her as she talked and show her that I was listening, encouraging her to keep going even when the words became difficult. Both of us sipped from the cokes. Once the bottle was empty my head was beginning to feel uncomfortably heavy on my arm and my cheek stuck to my palm with a slick of new sweat. She had her eyes closed most of the time so I thought it would be okay to put my head on the pillow too. When my eyelids also grew unbearably heavy I thought it might be a good idea to rest them, after all I could continue talking and listening.

By the time her husband showed up to see how we were doing the recorder lying between us had run out of tape and both of us were so deeply asleep we didn't even hear him coming into the room, only waking up when he sat down on the end of the bed and coughed politely.

An opportunist hack

When first attempting to find my way in the world as a writer I flirted with the idea that I should try to get a full-time post on a national paper or magazine.

An enterprising national journalist, who had taken on some public relations writing commissions for a Middle Eastern country, had found himself overloaded with work and hired me as a subcontractor. This was in the mid-seventies when cities like Dubai and Abu Dhabi were little more than immense building sites and the rest of the world was only just waking up to the fact that the people who lived there had become the richest on the planet, due to the revenues that were springing from their oil wells, and were going to be building entirely new and extraordinary metropolises where recently there had been little more than fishing villages.

Needing to pick up some papers from him I went to his office one day in Fleet Street and he introduced me to his surrounding colleagues. The atmosphere had all the noise, bustle and excitement that newspaper offices in Hollywood movies manage to reproduce and for a moment I wondered if this was where I should really be. The wide-eyed wonder with which I was looking around must have been obvious.

"So," one of the journalists asked as he waited with a phone clamped to his ear for someone to pick up at the other end, "are you hoping to get into a place like this, or are you just an opportunist freelance hack?"

The person at the other end of the line obviously picked up because he didn't wait for my answer, introducing himself and saying where he was calling from. The other person hung up.

Someone senior to the people I was sitting amongst burst into the room, hurling expletive-laden abuse in all directions. None of them seemed to be particularly bothered but all I could think was that I wanted to get back out into the fresh air and freedom of the street.

Walking home along Fleet Street I decided that I would stay on the outside a little longer, as far as possible from people who thought screaming abuse was a satisfactory way to pass the day and nowhere near anyone who was likely to hang up the phone as soon as they heard who I was.

A book goes global

Every week for about 15 years I continued to run the small ad in *The Bookseller* simply announcing "Ghost-writer for Hire" and giving my phone number. Sometimes months would pass with no responses and then a call would come which would set me off on a new adventure.

Towards the end of the eighties I received a cryptic call from a woman in Birmingham, who told me she had a friend who'd had a book written about her by a journalist, but who now wanted to tell the story from her own perspective. She wouldn't say any more, apart from the fact that she had been given my name by a librarian when she enquired how she should go about finding a ghost. The librarian had consulted a copy of *The Bookseller* that she happened to have under the counter.

Money was tight at the time and I had to decide whether such a vague lead was worth a train ticket all the way to Birmingham. Some instinct told me it would be, and anyway my curiosity had now been piqued. I wanted to find out what this story was.

In a small, crowded house I met Zana Muhsen, who told me how she and her sister, Nadia, had been sold by their father as child brides in the Yemen. It had taken their mother five years to find them and another couple of years to get Zana out. Nadia and their children were still trapped down there and Zana wanted to write a book that would draw attention to their plight and help them to escape.

It seemed like a great story, almost a classic fairy tale. Two innocent young girls imprisoned in a frightening, alien, exotic culture and then the tense story of Zana's escape. I wrote a synopsis and sent it round to a few agents. John Pawsey, an agent then working on the South Coast, thought it looked like a "nice little package", and agreed to send it out to the London publishers.

Everyone turned it down except for one, who offered us a few thousand pounds, which we accepted gratefully. *Sold* was duly published as a rather cheaply printed paperback and sank with barely a trace. So far, so predictable. Chalk it up to experience and be grateful for an interesting experience, a few thousand pounds and a book with my name on the cover as the co-writer.

A few months later John Pawsey rang to say that a German publisher was interested in the story and would like to meet us. This time Zana came down to London and we met in the gentlemanly environs of John's club. The German was charming and offered us an advance five times the size of the British one. A few days later John rang again, could we come to a meeting with a French publisher, then a Dutch one, and so it rolled on. Over the next few years the book came out in about nine different languages. It went to the top of the bestseller charts in all the countries it came out in. It became France's bestselling book of the year and Zana was feted in Paris as a cause célèbre.

John was able to go back to the British publishers and remind them that they owned this property and had possibly not exploited its full potential. Amazingly, they agreed and reissued it as a handsome hardback.

Just over 20 years since that first telephone call we have sold more than 5 million copies of the book around the world and I still get emails most days from readers telling me that they have just discovered it or that it is their favourite book ever, and asking what happened to Zana and Nadia after the end of the book. I am able to tell them that Nadia and the children are now free to travel to England.

It just goes to show, fairy tales can happen, even in the world of publishing.

Revenge can be bitter

I believe that one of the reasons *Sold* was so popular was Zana's lack of bitterness in the telling of the story. She might have been angry with her father and the other men who had held her and her sister as virtual prisoners for so many years, but she was not looking for revenge.

Many people decide they want to write books in order to get their own back on someone, desperate to tell their side of a disputed story, but such motives never make a story enticing to readers or publishers.

Some people want to attack their parents for cruelties that they believe were inflicted on them in childhood. Some want to get back at spouses and partners who deserted or betrayed them. Some want to expose the wrongdoings of petty officials or lawyers or big corporations or neighbours who have made their lives hell. None of these tales of woe will hold the sympathy of a reader for long.

Private grievances that might catch a reader's attention for 500 words in a newspaper, which they have bought already, will not necessarily tempt the same person to spend several pounds and several hours of their life to read at greater length in book form.

Bitterness is not attractive and it certainly doesn't work if it is stretched out over 200 or 300 pages. Courage, understanding and forgiveness are always more attractive to readers and generally make the teller of the story feel better about themselves at the same time. The moral high ground always provides a more attractive view of the world.

The Princess speaks

The Princess wanted to meet at Claridge's.

"We could have tea," she suggested, "and no one will know what we are talking about."

She had already told me that she had read *Sold* and one or two other books that I had written.

"I think the world needs to understand that these problems afflict women from all levels of society," she said, "not just those at the bottom. I think perhaps it might even be worse for the women like me in royal families. There is even more control; even more restrictions. We can talk about all these things when we meet."

The Princess had enjoyed a great many privileges. She was educated at an American university and she held down a good job within the government of her country, but she had still had to fight — sometimes actually trading physical blows — against male members of her family who had wanted to marry her to a man from another royal family, and who did not approve of the way she lived or dressed or talked.

"I am one of the lucky ones," she said as a waiter poured out the tea, "one of the ones who have been able to escape. Most are not so lucky. My mother never even went to school. She cannot read a word."

My experience over the coming years was to bear this out. A fellow ghost once told me of a client in a similar position to the Princess who hired her and they managed to get all the way to a completed manuscript, with the support of her apparently benevolent husband. When the moment came to publish, however, he put his foot down and the ghostwriter did not hear from her again. I guess he had been humouring his wife all along, not believing that she would ever get as far as talking to publishers. I did not hear from my Princess again either.

Confessions of my infidelity

When I set out to become a writer in the early seventies literary agents were no more than fantasy figures to me. I had no idea who they were or how I might find one to help me. I imagined that once I did locate one, however, he or she would take me under their wing in much the same way that Colonel Tom Parker had looked after Elvis, and they would do everything to launch me that Brian Epstein had done for the Beatles. Surely, I reasoned, literary agents must work in the same way as these infamous Svengalis of the music business, who we read so much about in the "Swinging Sixties".

Eventually I discovered where these mysterious agents' addresses and telephone numbers lay hidden and I started to pursue and plague them with letters and synopses and ideas and manuscripts. I was a frustrated and deluded stalker in pursuit of the ideal soulmate who I fantasised would accompany and support me through my professional life journey, assisting me in picking up all the glittering prizes along the way.

After what seemed like for ever one of them broke free of the ranks of rejection and indifference that had till then greeted my lovesick overtures, and agreed to take on the project I had sent to woo them. When they sold it I experienced an almost overwhelming surge of joy and tearful relief and assumed this was the start of my meteoric rise to fame and fortune, just like Elvis and the Beatles. But the next set of ideas I sent my beloved new agent didn't seem to catch her fancy. I could see I was losing her attention. What should I do? Should I scream and cry and make a scene? Should I sulk and pout? Should I beg?

Then it occurred to me that just because she didn't fancy my ideas, that didn't mean another agent wouldn't be interested. I wrote to tell her that if she wasn't interested I wouldn't just be chucking my work away, I would try to find another partner who would appreciate me more than she did. She replied that she was hurt by this betrayal. I pointed out that I had to live and I had managed to leave myself with no other skill in life than writing with which to support myself. This was a matter of basic survival. I promised always to bring projects to her for first refusal. She told me if she couldn't have me to herself then the relationship was over and I had a sickening feeling that I had made a terrible mistake.

But then another agent took one of the rejected ideas and managed to sell it, and yet another agent came to me with a project that had landed on their desk and needed a ghost and some royalties dribbled in from the book sold by agent number one, who resumed a semi-amicable relationship with me as a result. I realised that if I wanted to take advantage of every opportunity that came along, and if I wanted to exploit every idea and lead that came my way, I was going to have to run my professional life like an open marriage.

I returned to writing begging and submission letters with renewed gusto. Hundreds a week would fly out from my garret to the desks and bins of the literary world; no agent, publisher or editor was safe from my constant entreaties.

Most of the agents I started relationships with accepted that an open relationship would work well for both of us. If one complained that they really wanted me to work exclusively for them I had an answer ready: "If you can find me three or four books a year I won't have time to work for anyone else." Now and again one of them would manage to do that for a year or two. The trick was to retain their friendship whenever that particular seam of gold ran out and I had to return to looking for new pastures.

It wasn't long before I was set on a path of lifelong professional promiscuity.

How can anyone write
four books a year?

There are a number of stages to writing a book, each of which takes a great deal of time. You have to research it, you have to plot the whole thing out in your head, you have to write it, you have to sell it to an agent or a publisher and you then have to promote it to the potential readers. For most writers one, or at the most two, books a year are more than enough.

If you are ghostwriting, however, several of those stages are removed.

The research nearly always comes from one place — the author's head or filing cabinet. The structure generally becomes clear during the research period, meaning you can go straight to the writing and seldom have problems with "writer's block", a condition which usually occurs when you are trying to force yourself to write before you are ready with the material. The ghosted book will also probably be an easier sell to agents and publishers, although not always, and you do not have to be involved in any of the promotional activity which happens months after the writing is finished, allowing you to get straight on with the next book without interruption.

As a result you can be actually writing any day that you are not meeting with the client, which gives you far more writing time than if you are originating all the material yourself from a variety of sources and then trying to sell it to the world.

Waking up in the orphanage

Upon waking up in the orphanage I was assailed by a sickening sense of déjà vu, although I knew I had never been there before that night. I had never even been to Croatia before. There were the echoing sounds of children shouting, doors slamming, feet running on hard floors. The smells of institutional cooking mingled with those of disinfectant and economy cleaning fluids.

The orphanage had only just re-emerged from the rubble of a bombsite and the floor I was on was yet to be inhabited by children, which was how I was able to find a bed for a few nights. The bathrooms were brand new, clinically and spotlessly clean, but still had that communal feel about them, the rows of basins and showers threatening an invasion of privacy at almost every turn.

The return of this place from the ashes was a miracle of optimism, which was why I was there. My client had been instrumental in restoring it after enemy shells had all but destroyed it. The debris from wave upon wave of ethnic cleansing had been eradicated by a mixture of sheer hard work and good-heartedness. The restored orphanage now stood as a beacon of hope amidst the ruins of the beautiful old spa town. My client would turn out to be something of a saint, albeit with a twinkle in his eye, which had landed him in more than one controversy, and had also landed him a blue-chip publishing deal.

So why was there this sinking feeling in the pit of my stomach as I rose from my bed in the sparse dormitory and prepared to go in search of breakfast?

Then I remembered my first morning at boarding school; seven years old, away from home for the first time and terrified of the new, unknown world my parents had left me in. But I came from a privileged world, where people could afford to pay school fees and my parents would return at the end of term to pick me up and take me back to the security of the home I longed for so painfully whenever I was parted from it. There had been no bombs or gunfire to be heard in my childhood. The abandoned and abused inhabitants of this building had no such luxuries and no such hopes to cling to.

Pulling myself together I made my way downstairs to be engulfed by a crowd of the bolder children, all jabbering at me at once, while the more timid stared, wide eyed, at the stranger who had appeared in their midst, entirely unable to communicate with him beyond the odd gleefully shouted references to English pop singers and footballers that every child in the world seems to know.

The resulting book was a reasonable success. It was dramatised for television and the author became the subject for a tear-jerking episode of *This is Your Life*.

Some of the orphans whom he helped at the beginning are now adults telling their own stories of their interrupted childhoods.

Under armed guard in Lahore

It was an unusual ghosting project because the main character was 12 years old and had recently been assassinated. The story could have been narrated by a second person, but he was in hiding somewhere in Europe and was not at all sure he wanted to raise his head above the parapet in this way.

The project had been sparked into life by a producer who wanted to make a film about the life of Iqbal Masih, a Pakistani boy who had allegedly been sold by his parents to a carpet factory owner at the age of four. Six years later, the story went, he succeeded in escaping the clutches of his tyrannical master. A young boy alone in the world, surviving off foraged scraps, he stumbled across a Bonded Labour Liberation Front (BLLF) rally. The organisation took him under its wing, and he began working to spread the word to other enslaved children that they too could be free. He participated in raids on illegal factories and addressed international conventions. He was awarded the Reebok "Youth in Action" Award and a scholarship to study law in Boston. But before he could start to enjoy the results of his hard work, his life was cut short by a hail of bullets from the gun of an unknown sympathiser or employee of the carpet masters. Ehsan Khan, who ran the BLLF, had been forced to leave the country or face a similar fate, or imprisonment, and was now hiding in Europe.

"I want to make a film of Iqbal's life but I think there should be a book to go with it," the producer told me over lunch at the Rib Room, a haunt of the international rich in the Jumeirah Carlton Tower Hotel in London's Sloane Street. He was an imposing man, dressed completely in black, right down to his Gucci cowboy boots. "You need to come over to Lahore and see the village where he came from, the factory where he was enslaved and the place where they murdered him. You need to talk to his mother and to the people at BLLF. We will need to arrange for protection."

At our next meeting in the Rib Room Ehsan Khan was also there, emerging unannounced from his hiding place for a few hours to talk about the project, preparing the way for our trip. After lunch Ehsan hurried away, vanishing into the crowds as I strolled with the producer to Harrods where he wanted to pick up some of his favourite cigars.

"I will make all the travel arrangements," he said as we walked. "My brother-in-law is the chief of police in Lahore. He will provide us with the security we need."

It was decided a friend and co-worker of Ehsan's would come with us.

A week or two later we were ensconced in the Pearl-Continental Hotel in Lahore and news reached us over a sumptuous breakfast buffet, via the producer's luxury Vertu mobile, that all the campaign staff of BLLF had been arrested and were being held somewhere where we could not get access to them.

"I have talked to my brother-in-law," the producer said, "and he will see what he can do."

Later that morning we were taking coffee with the brother-in-law in his office, overlooking the overgrown courtyard of the colonial-style police station. The atmosphere in the office was relaxed as the two men seemed to gossip about friends and family, and perhaps talked a little about our plans for the coming week. Excluded by the language barrier, entirely reliant on them for everything, I settled down to await developments.

A shiny black Range Rover was found for us; the sheer size and splendour of it, I was assured, would be enough to intimidate anyone who might prefer not to see us in their village — and an armed guard was added to our entourage. There were reports that the imprisoned BLLF campaigners were being beaten somewhere in the bowels of the police station, which caused the producer consternation, but his brother-in-law merely shrugged to demonstrate his helplessness in the face of such inevitable injustice.

The streets of Lahore were hot and exciting, with a hint of threat in the stares that followed us wherever we went. Outside the city the Pakistani and Indian armies were lining their tanks up along either side of the border. In the villages the children and buffaloes splashed and wallowed in the red waters of the canals and rivers as the adults sat around watching the world in much the same way they must have been doing for centuries.

Everyone we came across wanted to tell us their side of the Iqbal story, playing up their own role in the drama, enjoying the break we were providing in their usual daily routines. Iqbal was both a local hero and already something of a mythical figure. It was becoming increasingly hard to tell the fantasies from the realities in everything we were being told.

The whole village seemed to be congregating in the school building where we went to meet more people who claimed they had known him. The crowd spilled out into the street, peering in through the door and windows at us. Overcome with emotion at one point, the producer made the mistake of opening his wallet to distribute largesse and the policeman had to insert himself and his rifle between us and the villagers as they pressed forward with their hands outstretched.

In the evenings we paid visits to a number of the producer's family members, and one of his mother's servants joined us, falling asleep in the back of the car and snoring loudly as we continued to travel to the brick kilns and carpet factories where whole families still work in virtual slavery, and out into the desolate fields where our little hero was murdered, watched from a distance by suspicious eyes as flocks of crows circled noisily in the air above us.

Iqbal's legend has all the elements of a classic fairy tale, a folk story that can be passed from mouth to mouth, growing and mutating as it goes. It was becoming almost impossible to see where the facts of the story might be but the fundamental truth about bonded child labour was becoming abundantly clear, just as it was in Europe and America in the days when children worked long hours in factories and mines and were sent up chimneys. The story of this one little boy who became a martyr made it more human and more understandable, just as Oliver Twist made Charles Dickens's message about the workhouses and orphanages of Victorian London more accessible and memorable. A drama teacher at an American school recently contacted me to ask if he could dramatise the book for a performance by his pupils, so maybe one day in the future Iqbal too will be the subject of a West End/Broadway musical.

Later I read *The Reluctant Fundamentalist* by Mohsin Hamid, where the complex characters frequented the Pearl-Continental Hotel and the same cafés and streets that I had travelled through with the producer. I smelled again the dangers that mine every cross-cultural encounter in modern Pakistan, feeling grateful for whatever protection it was the producer's brother-in-law gave us.

The tentative handling of firearms

"Take it," my ebullient host insisted, thrusting the lovingly oiled and polished shotgun (almost certainly not the correct name for it, but certainly what it looked like) into my hands. "Feel the weight."

I confirmed that I could feel the weight all too well. My previous experience of handling firearms had been limited to shooting lessons with Colonel Molesworth at prep school, which I only signed up to in order to get out of games at least one day a week, and firing an air rifle from a bedroom window at rabbits which threatened my wife's vegetable patch and magpies which she had caught attacking the house-martin nests that cling to the eaves of the house, and which she believes we have a moral responsibility to protect from all aggressors.

"Let's take it outside," my host suggested, ignoring my obvious eagerness to put the thing down as quickly as possible, steering me out with a firm, brotherly arm around the shoulders. "Go on," he said once we stood in the heat of the sun, "fire it."

I protested a few times but he was my host and a powerful personality. I was also beginning to feel wimpier than even I was comfortable with. I did as he instructed, the noise almost blowing my head off and the recoil digging painfully into my shoulder. As I returned to reality, my ears still ringing and the explosion still echoing off the distant mountains, I saw that he had a camera in his hand.

A few weeks later, when safely back in England, my host sent me some prints of the pictures.

"What are these?" my wife asked, picking them up from where I had put them aside. "Are they from the Pakistan trip?"

"Yes," I replied, feeling an all too familiar prickle of disquiet.

"What's with the gun?"

"Oh, just messing around." I tried to sound so casual that she would lose all interest in her line of questioning, and failed.

"So," she said as if recapping for a particularly dim schoolboy, "these are pictures of you posing in one of the most politically volatile places on earth with a particularly lethal-looking firearm? And someone else has the negatives? Was that a good idea?"

"Well, obviously, when you put it like that . . ."

The faulty memories of rock gods

The approach came at the end of a lunchtime talk at the Biographers' Club, as everyone was moving towards the cloakrooms, some exchanging business cards, others hurrying off to their next appointments, all of us having tarried too long over a gossipy meal. A rock journalist of senior years, who had several music biographies under his belt, introduced himself and came quickly to the point.

"I have a friend," he said, "who was a big rock star in the sixties and early seventies. He was absolutely at the centre of the business and knew everyone who was anyone during that period, not just the music people but the artists and the writers and the fashion designers, the whole 'Swinging London' scene. There have been a few problems and he's a bit down on his luck. He wants to write an autobiography but there's no way he would be able to do it himself. I'm not even sure he can read — probably dyslexic or something. He keeps asking me to help, but to be honest I think I've known him too long. It needs someone to come at it fresh and catch his voice."

"What sort of problems has he had?" I asked.

"Well," he avoided my eyes as he took his coat from the cloakroom attendant, "there have been a few issues. He's not been brilliant with the money and he has a few bad habits . . ."

"Drink? Drugs? Gambling? Sex?" I tried to prompt him to be a little more specific.

"Umm." He made a non-committal sound which seemed more affirmative than not.

"All of them?"

"Well, you know. It was the sixties and . . ." he shrugged his coat on, "would you just talk to him? Give him a bit of guidance on what his options might be?"

Stories from people who were insiders in London at that period are always intriguing. It was a time when the Beatles and all the others were changing the music scene for ever and people like Mary Quant and Vidal Sassoon were changing the way we all looked. It was an era that seemed revolutionary and exciting at the time and with the passing years had also taken on a patina of historical interest as well. To be honest I was already hooked.

The call came and we agreed to meet at his home in World's End, Chelsea. It was a council-owned flat in a shabby Victorian block with gloomy brick stairwells that reeked of urine and echoed with a mixture of hostile sounds. Inside, the flat was surprisingly bare. The rock star lived alone like any other old man on a meagre pension, surrounded by the simple necessities of existence. It was a perfectly safe and clean little flat, but gave no hint that the old boy with the bad haircut, who seldom moved from his armchair with an ashtray balanced on the arm, apart from going to the pub, had once been adored by millions, playing live to crowds of thousands and reputedly sleeping with hundreds.

By the time I met him I had already checked the idea with an agent, who told me that if the stories were sufficiently star-studded we would almost certainly be able to get him a deal because there would be potential for a lucrative newspaper serialisation. At that stage several of the richest newspapers were waging circulation wars and were paying sums for book extracts that dwarfed anything that the publishers were willing to shell out.

Pete was extremely affable, especially if we were in a bar, and full of stories that didn't quite lead to anything but were enough to put together a synopsis which hooked a major publisher. When someone has a fund of anecdotes people in pubs will inevitably tell them that they "should write a book", but anecdotes alone will not hold a reader's attention for 200 or more pages. Pete had absolutely no powers of description and no emotional insight into himself or anyone else that he had ever met. He would greet any questions I might have with an entirely uncomprehending stare, before launching back into another anecdote. Despite all that, however, he had led an amazing life and I was sure there was a story in the meteoric rise and fall of his star.

"Why don't you give me a list of 20 people you hung out with during those years," I suggested after one particularly long and fruitless session with the tape machine, "and I'll go round and see what they have to say, like I would if I was writing a biography. Then I'll put everything back into your words."

Sometimes the partner or friend of someone famous can provide greater insights into their worlds than the central characters themselves. Kathy Etchingham, for instance, met Jimi Hendrix on his first night in England in 1966. She became his girlfriend, living with him in Mayfair's Brook Street and remaining his friend until his death in 1970. During those four years he rose from being unknown to being a legend of the music industry and Kathy was an integral part of that scene, a period when British groups like the Beatles and the Animals (and Pete) were making music history. I had helped her to capture the period in general as well as the intimate details of Hendrix's short life in her memoir *Through Gypsy Eyes*, painting a picture of a life that no one else had experienced, and the resulting book had worked well. It seemed likely to me that if I could find some witnesses as good as Kathy I would be able to bring Pete's world to life on the page in the same way.

His obvious relief at being given an escape route from my continual questioning resulted in him pulling together a list of names which was like a who's who of Swinging London. Most of them were old enough to now have some time on their hands and would enjoy reminiscing about their glory days. They all had fond memories of their times with Pete and were happy to talk about him at length. The ruse, it seemed, was working.

I collected together all the stories and ran them by Pete, who happily confirmed all of them, often embellishing them even further. We were off and running. The newspaper deal was done, the book was printed up and was scheduled to go into the shops the second day of the newspaper serialisation.

The night before the first part was due to appear in the paper I bumped into one of the people who had supplied me with stories and he enquired how the project was going and who else I had seen after him. I named someone who was a good friend of his as well as Pete's.

"Really," he said. "How is he? He will have told you some porkies."

"You think?" I laughed, assuming he was teasing.

"Absolutely," he said, "but then I told you a fair few porkies too."

"Did you?" I think my laugh may now have carried the slightest touch of hysteria.

"Yes," he said, his accompanying chuckle entirely hysteria-free. "But none of the porkies he and I told you will be anything to the ones Pete will have dished up."

Frozen is probably what my smile was by that stage. The book was printed and crated and heading towards the back doors of bookshops all over the country. Would this be the moment to ring the publisher and report this little conversation? I decided it would make me sound alarmist, maybe even naive. Best to hold on and see what happened. Maybe he was just kidding.

The following morning the first part of the serialisation was splashed across the middle pages of the paper, flagged up mightily on the front page. A few hours later lawyers' letters began to be delivered to the newspaper's offices suggesting that some of the stories were entire fabrications and enquiring what the editor intended to do about it.

The editor intended to get very cross indeed as it turned out. The publisher was hauled over the coals and rang Pete, who cheerfully denied all knowledge of any of the stories he was being challenged on. Fortunately, I had all our conversations on tape and could prove that I had not made any of it up. The books were recalled and pulped, everyone apologised to everyone and Pete went to the pub that evening as if nothing had happened. For him it was just one more incident in a life full of such incidents, another anecdote to be told to his mates, who could then roar with laughter and slap him merrily on the back.

Really, the old boy should write a book.

Soldiers' tales

Two soldiers with stories to tell arrived in my life in one week. One was a man who had joined up to serve his country and support his young wife and child after leaving school without many qualifications. His short, brave adventure in a foreign land had left him a shaking wreck, trying to survive on an inadequate disability pension. We met in a pub where he was hardly able to lift his pint to his lips without spilling it. The second soldier was a smart little officer who was chauffeured to our lunch date at the Ritz. Since leaving the British Army he had become notorious for building a highly profitable mercenary force which was rumoured in some quarters to use "excessive force". I'd met prefects like him at school and had always made sure to give them a wide berth, but I thought it would be interesting to find out what he had been up to — a sort of real-life Flashman.

One of these soldiers talked with painful honesty about his experiences while the other was evasive, constantly alluding to things that he "couldn't talk about", and apparently very pleased with himself. Neither of them was anything like any of the stereotypical British soldiers I had been brought up to expect.

Having had a "good war", my parents were very well disposed towards the armed forces. Many of my relatives were full-time servicemen who had reached high ranks. I had read *Biggles* (albeit not enjoying his escapades as much as the Scarlet Pimpernel's and Dr Syn's), and watched John Mills, David Niven, Kenneth More and other British gents behaving very finely in the black and white films we were shown at school on alternate Saturday evenings during the winter terms. Many centuries of romantic tales of noble knights and fearless warriors provided the building blocks for the mythical figures that were paraded before us then, and those that still stride around the imaginations of new generations in the militaristic computer games that sell by the million.

No one, it seemed from listening to these two soldiers and several others who came forward to tell their stories in the wake of successful authors like Andy McNab and Chris Ryan, had had anything close to a "good war" since 1945.

The horror of guerrilla warfare and improvised explosive devices, the bullying by the Americans with their "Napalm in the morning" in Vietnam and "shock and awe" in Iraq, and the relentless crushing of every small country that stood in the way of the Soviet military machine, had left men with terrible tales that were very different to anything I had heard or read during my childhood.

After being part of a highly successful operation in Iraq, Andy McNab and Chris Ryan had both turned their personal "knights' tales" into bestselling thrillers and themselves into publishing brands. A great many other soldiers strove to follow the same path. Meanwhile senior officers who would once have written dry battlefield accounts with stiff upper lips were forced by modern readers' tastes to talk more about the emotional side of warfare and soldiering, draining still further the heroic myths that had grown so powerful during the first half of the twentieth century, with the help of Hollywood.

The public will always want heroes but now they expect believable, rounded ones. It's all right for soldiers to talk about fear and pain and missing their families, just as it is all right for other people to talk about unhappy childhoods in other autobiographies. Heroes now tend to be mavericks rather than "military machines" as they might once have been proud to be known. The recruiters can no longer expect to get away with the same blatant, one-dimensional propaganda they might have been able to use a hundred years ago because the potential Western soldier is more knowing, better educated and has become able to show a more human face to the world just as warfare itself has become more technological and less human.

The potential power of these modern soldiers' stories, however, did not escape the notice of the Ministry of Defence, who called me into their inner sanctum to meet one particular man whose story they felt summed up the modern stresses and strains of soldiering particularly well. He and I were sucked in through one security zone after another until we found ourselves sitting together in a room, which felt distinctly padded, with a coffee machine and a code number should we want to escape back out onto the street.

I liked him and I liked the story so I prepared a synopsis for them as requested. The publishers we approached, however, smelled a propaganda rat and did not take the bait.

Win a ghost of your own

It's always a treat to receive unexpected calls from editors in large publishing houses. If they have got as far as looking up your number and picking up the phone the chances are that they have something genuinely interesting to offer. This voice, however, sounded slightly less confident than such august folk usually are when planning to dispense largesse to hungry authors.

"Ummm," she said, "I don't know how you will feel about this, but . . ." I was on the edge of my seat to know what was coming next, "we're setting up a competition for viewers of *Richard & Judy* to send in their stories and the three winners are going to be given a publishing deal . . ." she hesitated again, ". . . and a ghostwriter."

This was a time when Richard and Judy, the king and queen of afternoon sofa television, were at the peak of their success and were running a book club on air, which was making bestsellers of books that would previously have been lucky to earn out their advances. Their muscle in the UK publishing industry (or at least their producer's muscle) was comparable to *Oprah*'s influence over the US publishers. In fact, their producer was frequently named as the most powerful person in publishing.

"Would you be at all interested in taking that on?" she finished.

"So," I said, wanting to be entirely sure that I understood the deal on offer here, "you have no idea what the stories will be about or how good they will be?"

"None at all," she laughed nervously.

"So it's possible you won't get anything that could remotely be described as a potential book?"

"That is a risk. There is also a risk that we will be inundated by tens of thousands of stories and we will have to read through them all. It's all a bit of a risk."

"So who will do the judging?"

"The public."

"The public?"

"Well, we'll be narrowing it down to six finalists and then they will vote for the one they want to win."

"But the public might vote for something which is great in a five-minute television segment but has no back story that we can draw on to build a narrative . . ."

"Like I say," she gave another nervous laugh, "a bit of a risk."

"I'd love to," I said because I am a freelancer and freelancers are hard-wired never to say no to an offer of work just in case they never get another one, and I actually rather relished the challenge of taking whatever stories were given to me and finding ways of spinning them out to book length.

The "True" competition was announced (Judy sweetly described part of the prize as being the services of "a world class ghostwriter") and the entries poured in. People in the publisher's office and the producer's office started the sorting process and the best ones were filmed and made into items for the show. The public then voted. By that stage the publisher had realised that asking one ghost to write all three books in the sort of timeframe they would need if they wanted to publish while the public still remembered the competition was perhaps a little unrealistic. Instead, I was contracted to write two of them and someone else would handle the third.

As it turned out there were three strong winners and the overall champion became *Betrayed*, which I wrote for Lyndsey Harris. For the first few years of her life Lyndsey's daughter, Sarah (not their real names), was a normal, happy, popular girl. But from the age of six she was targeted by a vicious, manipulative but invisible enemy — and her life became a living hell. Before long she was suspended from school, alienated from her friends, completely bewildered and utterly terrified. Her happy childhood had been destroyed for ever. For Lyndsey it was a life beyond her worst nightmares. Her little girl, the daughter she loved so much, seemed to have transformed overnight — into a child she hardly recognised, stealing razor blades, trying to poison her friends, accusing her parents of abuse. Suddenly Lyndsey was fighting to keep her family together and to save her daughter's sanity. But then the horrific truth started to become clear, and both Lyndsey and Sarah discovered they had been the innocent victims of the most horrifying betrayal imaginable . . .

Betrayed went straight to the top of the bestseller charts. Richard and Judy had triumphed yet again.

The runner-up, which I also ghosted, was *Shattered* by Mavis Marsh, whose son, Matthew, fell off a roof just as he was about to graduate from university and start a glittering career. After a year in a coma he defied the predictions of the medical profession and started to respond, although nothing in the family's lives would ever be the same again.

Selling your story to a magazine

Many of the people who contact me about ghostwriting services have great stories to tell but they can be told in just a few thousand words, and they are probably not something that the reading public would be willing to pay for in isolation. There can, however, be a market for these stories in magazines and there are ghostwriters who actively seek them out.

The downside is that you don't have much control over how the stories are presented. If the magazine editor decides to add a gruesome headline or picture, or wants to cut it to fit the magazine layout, there is little you can do about it. You will also only get paid a few hundred pounds (if you get paid at all). If none of these things strike fear into your heart, however, then it is one way of getting your story out there and might be a first step towards getting a full-scale book deal, although probably not.

Often when people approach me about the possibility of me ghosting for them, they will supply an article which has already been written about them. Zana and Nadia Muhsen, for instance, had had their story told initially by *The Observer*, and then picked up by every other newspaper. Those articles helped me to see the overall structure of the story which eventually grew to become *Sold*. In other cases, however, the fact that a story can be neatly summed up in 500 or a thousand words indicates that there may not be enough material to hold the reader's attention for another 70,000 or more words.

Calls from out of the blue

These days most of my adventures start with an email, but in the mid-nineties they still arrived by telephone, and they could come from any time zone, night or day.

"Mr Crofts," the distant voice asked as I picked up the phone, jerked painfully awake by its alarming ring, "do you like coming to the Far East?"

"Yes," I replied, expecting to be told next that I should buy a time-share overlooking Pattaya beach.

"I'm working for a very successful businessman," he continued, "in Kuala Lumpur. He is thinking of writing his autobiography."

Once I had shaken my thoughts into place one thing led to another and a month or two later I found myself ensconced in a five star hotel in Kuala Lumpur, waiting to meet the founder and chief executive of one of Malaysia's most successful banks. A private dining room had been booked and he swept into the lobby exactly on time, at the head of an entourage galloping to keep up. Over lunch he talked while we chewed on chickens' feet, watched by the silently munching entourage around the circular table.

It was a good story. His father had come from China with nothing more than a rush mat rolled up under his arm, working on the rubber plantations as a coolie. The banker had started his working life as a child tapping rubber from high up on the trunks of the trees with flaming torches strapped to his head during the hours of darkness, frequently singeing his hair off.

Now he lived amongst all the trappings you would expect of one of the richest and most successful people in a city which was at the forefront of what was then being called the "Tiger Economy". We got on well and he hired me for the job. It meant spending many hours with him in the city, but also travelling to the jungle village where he'd been born and brought up. He answered every question openly but I couldn't help feeling that there was something else to the story that I wasn't being told.

He was widely feted around town and found the attention mildly embarrassing. There was one particular dinner at a fancy hotel where the hosts insisted on ordering an expensive bottle of wine just for him, despite his protests, while the rest of the party drank something more modest.

"I don't like that," he muttered as we left at the end of the meal, "but what can you do? People want to do things for you."

During the course of us writing the book the "Tiger Economy" crashed. There were reports in the papers that the banker was now worth many billions of dollars less than he had been when I first met him, but I didn't see any discernible change in his lifestyle.

After several trips to KL, I was getting close to finishing the book when he announced he was coming to London and invited me to his hotel in Grosvenor Square for lunch. I was shocked to be greeted by a man with only a few wisps of hair on his head where just a few weeks before he had sported a lustrous black mop.

"At home I have to wear a wig," he explained when he saw my eyes flickering to the top of his head. "If word got out that I was ill it would affect the business."

"You're ill?"

With that announcement a number of things became clear, particularly the urgency with which he now wanted to see the project finished. The hair loss was due to chemotherapy and that lunch was the last time I saw him alive. The book was published in Singapore and was a fitting memorial to the man and his achievements. Without him there to promote it, however, it was never likely to reach an audience much wider than his friends, family and business associates.

I am an addict

I confess I am addicted to chasing possibilities for interesting new experiences.

They might be delivered in the form of a phone call out of the blue or, more often these days, as an email pinging into the inbox or a message through one of the social media sites. Then there are the voice mails (or answering machine messages as they once were), and the anxiety that comes from the terrible fear of missing some fascinating opportunity and the craving to be both distracted from that worry and reassured that I am still learning new things at a rate that will keep the addiction satisfied.

The seeds of a new story are usually unfamiliar and unexpected; on the phone it might be a foreign accent that is hard to understand (always promising), or the email might come from an unknown name at an unknown address and convey a cryptic enquiry without giving any further information. As long as there is something unknown in the offing there is a possibility of an adventure unfurling. It could be an invitation into a home or boardroom that I would otherwise be excluded from, an airline ticket to Bangkok or Haiti,

New York or Rio, or just the promise of a story that will make my toes curl in anticipation.

The "hit" and rush of optimism comes from the hope that something diverting is approaching, something intriguing and different, an experience that will open my eyes to something I didn't know before.

More often than not, of course, a ringing phone merely yields up a domestic crisis or a sales call from some other person desperately searching the ether for someone who will be interested in whatever they have to sell, and there is a momentary spasm of disappointment as I realise this call isn't going to provide any sort of high. Most emails will be spam or mundane or will quickly lead to a dead end, but the 24-hour, 7-day world that we now live in means that a golden nugget could appear from the mud at any time of the night or day. That is what makes it so tempting to check the emails at regular intervals, and to spring to answer the phone when it rings. Someone in LA could just be sitting down at their computer to type a note to me as I head up to bed; someone in Hong Kong could be ringing before dawn has even made it through my eyelids.

It is an addiction which provides a hit as pure and sweet as any narcotic. It numbs the reality of daily life just as effectively as alcohol, passes the time just as effectively as lighting another cigarette.

The next rush comes when I follow up the enquiry and my brain receives what feels like an impossibly heavy overload of unfamiliar information. I can't believe that I will ever be able to unravel it, give it shape and turn it into something digestible for readers, sharing my excitement of discovery with them. The adrenaline is made to flow. As the weeks and months go by, however, the fog of confusion begins to clear and I start to understand the subject. Finally I am ready to write, drifting gently back down to reality once more, and soon I am desperate for another hit from a new possibility for an adventure, either physical or mental.

Evangelists of technology

Can you remember the first time someone described the internet to you?

I guess you would have to have been born before 1980 to have had such a mind-blowing moment. Anyone younger would have imbibed the concept while suckling at their mother's breast, or soaked it up in the school classroom or playground. If, however, you were born before cyberspace was a generally understood concept there is almost bound to have been a memorable instant of revelation.

I had that "road to Damascus" moment at a writers' group where an evangelist from the then weird world of information technology came to explain to us what the world wide web was and how it was going to change our lives. I was still at the stage of being by far the youngest in any room filled with professional writers but even so I found it hard to grasp the full potential of what was being described to us. I'd only just got the hang of inserting floppy disks.

Every bit of information in the world would soon be available on my computer screen at the click of a button? Surely this was the stuff of wild science fantasy?

When I got home that night and my wife asked what the talk had been about I completely failed to convey any of the sense of mystery and excitement that the evangelist had managed to pump into the back room of the pub I'd been in a few hours earlier. I just couldn't get my head around the concept sufficiently to answer any of her incredulous questions.

"Perhaps," I thought as I lay in bed, staring at the ceiling and trying to imagine how I would ever be able to master something so potentially immense, "it will go away and I can just continue to bumble along with my Amstrad word processor, my fax machine and our revolutionary new cordless house phone."

"Mr Harris would like to quote you..."

Once your book has been given life and sailed out into the world to seek its fortune (and hopefully yours), there is no way of knowing whose hands it will end up in. Just occasionally, however, a bit of feedback arrives which takes you completely by surprise.

An email arrived in my inbox from the address of a well-known publisher. That's always a moment that lifts the heart for a few hopeful seconds.

I opened it to find a short message from an editor to tell me that he was about to publish Robert Harris's latest novel, which was going to be called *The Ghost*.

"The central character is a ghostwriter and Mr Harris would like to quote your ghostwriting handbook at the start of each chapter."

Robert Harris had read my handbook on ghostwriting? That was a concept that took a bit of getting used to. I was so shocked I said "yes" before I'd even thought of asking for any money. The kind publisher sent me a copy of the manuscript and it was brilliant — it was Robert Harris for heaven's sake. He had caught the ghostwriter's world exactly. He opened every chapter with a quote from my book, starting with: "Of all the advantages that ghosting offers, one of the greatest must be the opportunity that you get to meet people of interest."

Finding himself writing about a profession of which he knew little he had ordered a few books on the subject for research purposes. Mine had managed to catch his imagination and had helped him to picture the world of his leading (and unnamed) character.

Harris's book was controversial from the start because the media assumed that the other main protagonist — a former Prime Minister who had dragged the country into a fruitless war on the coat-tails of America and was now having his autobiography ghosted — was based on Tony Blair. It was well known that Harris had been a big supporter of Blair at the beginning but had become deeply disillusioned over Iraq (along with most of the country). Harris doggedly, and unconvincingly, denied the connection.

The publisher threw a mighty launch party in a stately club in St James's, packing it with famous media faces. Having been a BBC reporter before he was a bestselling author, it is quite possible that Harris is the best-connected novelist in the country.

Things went up a gear when Roman Polanski expressed an interest in turning it into a film. Ewan McGregor was cast as the ghost (no complaints there), and Pierce Brosnan was to play the Prime Minister. (I doubt if Tony Blair had any complaints about that particular bit of casting either, even though it was strongly denied that the Prime Minister character was based on him. What man would complain about being portrayed by James Bond?)

Another gale of publicity hit the film during production when Polanski was put under house arrest for the statutory rape charge that had been keeping him out of the States for more than 30 years. He and Harris continued to work on the film together from Polanski's chalet in Gstaad.

At a press preview of the final film in a private Soho cinema my wife leaned across to me after only a few minutes.

"Ewan McGregor's saying all the same things you say," she whispered.

Damn, should have asked for a fee.

A confession of conceit

I'm always banging on to journalists that one of the main attributes required for ghostwriting is that you need to be able to suspend your ego, and I certainly stand by it as a necessary part of the process. I have done a pretty good job over the years of keeping mine sedated, but I have to confess that there have been times, in between ghosting assignments, when my ego has broken through like one of those white stage tigers in Las Vegas that savaged their trainer, so this is a confession of those moments of conceit.

Seeing how successful the construction of Robert Harris's book, *The Ghost*, was, reinforced my own long-held belief that ghostwriters make excellent central characters and narrators for fictional adventures. Like policemen, private detectives, lawyers and doctors, their lives are made up of bite-sized dramatic episodes. Every time an enquiry comes in from a potential client you have the starting point for a plot, which can be wrapped up at the end with the publication (or shelving) of the book.

Following through on that theory I have twice written novels with ghostwriters as narrators. The first was *Maisie's Amazing Maids*, which drew on my experiences of human trafficking and the stories of bar girls I had met in the Far East, and was sold to a publisher called Stratus by Andrew Lownie, afterwards republished through his own imprint, Thistle. Later I wrote *Secrets of the Italian Gardener*, narrated by a ghostwriter who is working for a Middle Eastern dictator just as the Arab Spring awakens to topple him, an idea that came to me after taking tea with Mrs Mubarak and meeting other powerful figures in the region at that time.

I showed *Secrets of the Italian Gardener* to Robert Kirby at United Agents. Robert is an agent I have worked with a great deal over the years. He was the eager young assistant to the legendary agent Giles Gordon when he first responded to my "Ghostwriter for Hire" ad and went on to become one of the founders of United Agents, now amongst the biggest and most successful agencies in London. He was extremely encouraging over dinner in a restaurant in Soho's Tin Pan Alley. He told me it was, "a contemporary recasting of Ecclesiastes, a story about the vanity associated with the desire for power and possessions and ultimately about the cycle of birth, growth, death and rebirth" — which was a surprise, but by no means an unpleasant one. Fired up on food and wine we felt optimistic that we would be able to get a quick sale to a traditional publisher.

Six months later Robert had to admit that he had failed to convince any publishers to come into business with us on this one. In the old days that would have been the end of the story and the manuscript would have been consigned to a drawer somewhere, the wasted time written off to experience. Things had changed, however, and simple self-publishing was now an option. But I had heard of a new service from Amazon, which they were calling their "White Glove Service". This seemed to me to offer yet another, and to my mind far preferable, alternative.

It is my belief that almost all the innovations that Amazon has brought to/forced on the publishing and bookselling industries over the last couple of decades have eventually worked to the advantage of authors and readers. I am quite sure that if I were a publisher or a bookseller I would feel very differently about the rise of Amazon to virtual world dominance, but I'm not. As both an author and a reader I love the many ways in which they have enriched my life. They had created the White Glove Service in conjunction with established literary agents with a view to helping those agents to publish and promote books for their clients that they had been unable to persuade traditional publishers to take on, or which had fallen out of print.

Robert Kirby's assistant, Holly Thompson, an ex-publisher herself, proceeded to copy-edit the manuscript and then did all the heavy lifting with getting the book up onto Amazon, ready for print-on-demand as well as electronic publication, liaising with them about prices and promotions in a way that no author would ever be able to do on his or her own. The process provided several advantages over straightforward self-publishing because it meant the project had become a team effort rather than a lone author's voice in the crowd and should the book start to "gain traction" in the market place (and offers for film rights came in pretty quickly), one of the biggest agencies in London was already fully engaged and ready to handle the business side of taking it to the next level.

Once the book existed it started to garner good reviews. In the first promotion that Amazon included it in a few months later, it became Kindle's number one political book within a few days, apparently allowing it to enter into the black magic world of "improved metadata and algorithms", whatever that might mean.

Guilt and self-doubt

Much of my day is eaten up with feeling guilty that I am not doing enough of whatever it is I should be doing. I know that in order to earn a living I must put in a certain number of hours a day at the keyboard, which means that every hour that I spend making coffee, reading the paper, browsing the internet or faffing about in the garden is potentially "wasted".

I know that it is sensible to finish the book with the closest deadline before allowing myself to be distracted by the interesting new project which has just arrived and which is not yet earning any money, but often that temptation is impossible to resist. Then there is the guilt attached to not writing as many words as I think perhaps I should, or perhaps not editing them tightly enough, or the fear that perhaps I'm just not good enough to be earning my living as a writer at all.

All the time self-doubt is nagging away at the back of my mind, telling me that I have been lucky to get away with earning my living in such an enjoyable way for this long and sooner or later I am going to be exposed as a fraud and no more work will ever come my way.

When the children were small I felt guilty for not working hard enough to provide them with financial security, and then I felt guilty for always being away or distracted or locked in my office when I should have been giving them more attention, despite the fact that I stood on the sidelines of a million school netball matches and events involving horses and children doing incredibly dangerous-looking things, feeling guilty as I did so about the hours of potential work that were seeping away as I cheered on the offspring.

I feel guilty for having to work in the evening because I've procrastinated all day, and then I feel guilty for starting to write earlier in the day without putting as much thought and research into the project as perhaps I should have done.

Is it possible, however, that these sorts of guilt and self-doubt are the fuels which drive us, and that without them we would simply stay in bed all day watching television and ordering takeaways?

The awesome power of a tear on daytime television

The book I had written for my client was dribbling into the shops at the usual dismal speed, when the author was invited onto one of the morning television sofas. For a moment it looked like his nerves would not allow him to accept and it seemed that the publisher's publicity lady might well die of disappointment, but with a remarkable show of courage and much encouragement from his wife, he steeled himself and took the plunge.

Under the glare of the spotlights, the sweat prickling through his make-up, he told the story of his childhood and everything he had suffered at the hands of a cruel mother, following that up with a painful coming-of-age story.

His vulnerability struck a chord in the motherly heart of the famous presenter on the opposite couch. She looked as if she just wanted to envelop him in her arms and protect him from the world. The watching public must have felt the same. When she reached for a tissue and dabbed a tear from her eye the distribution machinery inside one of the mightiest and most prestigious publishers in the world awoke and stirred into action.

By the following morning there were stacks of the book in every shop and by the following Sunday it was top of the *Sunday Times* bestseller list.

An avalanche had been set in motion by a single tear on daytime television.

Christina Foyle, queen
of all she surveyed

When I arrived in London in 1970, a wide-eyed 17-year-old, Richard Nixon was in the White House, Edward Heath was taking over from Harold Wilson in Downing Street, the Beatles were breaking up and Foyles was the pre-eminent London bookshop by far.

It was huge, rambling and scruffy and so old-fashioned Dickens would not have looked out of place in any of its shambolic departments. The shortest route between floors was via a bare concrete stairwell which surrounded a clanking lift shaft. It had the most ridiculous payment system ever invented, involving queuing two or even three times at different counters, and a reputation for treating its employees as virtual, if willing, slaves.

Hovering over all this was a penthouse, the London home of the fragrant Christina Foyle (she had a fantastic, peacock-strewn country house as well), who had been working in the shop since 1928. Her father had founded the bookselling business with his brother in 1903; later they moved to Charing Cross Road. Her biggest claim to fame was the founding of the "Foyles Literary Lunches"; vast, glittering affairs held in the grandest hotel ballrooms of Park Lane, bringing "writers and thinkers" together with their readers. Virtually all the most famous names of the twentieth century ended up at one of these lunches eventually, either as performers or as guests on Miss Foyle's high table.

A few years later I was commissioned by a magazine to do a series of profiles of interesting London figures. Having just published my first novel (the publisher was a magnificently eccentric Nigerian by the name of Dillibe Onyeama, who had shot to fame with his own autobiography controversially entitled *Nigger at Eton*), I had personal reasons for wanting to meet this woman who ruled London's literary landscape. I made tentative enquiries of the bookshop staff, who were obviously puzzled by the very concept of something as vulgar as press relations but promised to pass my request on.

Eventually summoned to a conservatory in the penthouse for tea, I met a woman who seemed to me to be exactly as the Queen herself would be in such circumstances. Later, when Margaret Thatcher came to power, I realised I could also see elements of the same steely, handbag style of charm. It was like being granted an audience with a very grand great aunt, the sort of tea-party conversation I had watched my mother indulging in throughout my childhood. We sat amongst the palms, gazing out across the rooftops of Soho, sipping from wafer thin china cups. She asked me

142

gracious questions about my novel and politely assured me she would make sure it was well stocked in the shop. The interview ended and I wrote the piece.

A few months later an impressively stiff invitation arrived at my room in a shared flat in Earls Court, inviting me to sit on the high table at the next Foyles Literary Lunch. The format of these lunches was always the same. There would be one or two main speakers, who were usually people with potentially bestselling books to promote, and the rest of their long table would be filled with invited guests who tended to be people whom Miss Foyle knew or whom she was grooming for future events. All the other tables were filled with the paying customers, who came to eat, listen, buy books and have them signed. The people on the high table would all sit along one side and in my memory they were raised slightly higher than the rest to afford better visibility to the masses — but my memory may have become confused by artists' depictions of the Last Supper.

All of the denizens of the high table were famous and all of them were, conservatively speaking, at least three times my age. High table invitees were assembled in an anteroom first in order to be greeted and introduced and we made more polite small talk before being wheeled out to the adoring paying public. It was glorious, like stepping into the teachers' common room at Hogwarts; part of the last great hurrah for publishing elitism before the much-needed tidal wave of democratisation hit books and education and life in general. The age of deference was teetering on the brink of extinction, although it would prove to be a long-drawn-out demise, and a whole new world was arriving through the doors which had been thrown open by the pioneers of the sixties.

I received several more such invitations from Miss Foyle and I confess I accepted every one of them because it was a magical kingdom to visit, albeit a suffocating one to live in as a young man trying to break into what seemed like a closed and elite world.

Nearly 40 years later my wife and I received an invitation to one of the Queen's summer garden parties at Buckingham Palace.

"This'll be a bit of a test for all your wishy-washy republican opinions," she said when I showed her the invitation.

I didn't bother to struggle with my conscience for long. For so many years I had been forced to walk all the way round the giant slab of a building and its walled gardens whenever I wanted to get between Victoria Station and the West End that the temptation to see inside the walls was too much to resist, as it has been in any of the other palaces I have managed to infiltrate around the world over the decades.

As the Queen and her family descended the palace steps to mingle with the guests on the lawns I was struck by the fact that she was still dressed pretty much as Miss Foyle had been that day at tea. It was like being transported to a pleasantly landscaped time capsule, rolling green lawns filled with top hats, brass bands, tea tents, officers and bishops. Maybe not as much has changed as I would like to think.

A new breed of stars

As well as bombarding publishers and agents with letters offering my writing services in the early days, I also approached individuals and organisations that I found interesting and that I thought might like to commission books or articles. One of the earliest commissions I received as a result was from a drama school in South Kensington called the Webber Douglas Academy of Dramatic Art. It had been the training ground for a number of stars including both Julian Fellowes, who went on to create *Downton Abbey*, and Hugh Bonneville who played the lead in the series.

Founded in 1926 the school evolved from being the hobby of two gentlemen from good families who had an interest in music and drama (particularly opera), to being one of the main drama schools in London. My task was to interview as many people as possible who were still alive in order to write a history. The interviewees ranged from a grand old lady called Dolly who received me for tea at her stately Kensington home wearing a tea gown, to Terence Stamp, who was part of the new generation of young working-class actors then becoming global stars. Although proudly working class and previously a flat-mate to Michael Caine, Stamp was by then living in an apartment in the Albany, Piccadilly, and suggested we meet for tea across the road at Fortnum & Mason, where he was a regular customer.

The sixties may have witnessed a social revolution, but the old world of the London Establishment, epitomised by Christina Foyle and Dolly in her tea gown, still held an enduring appeal for those who could afford to join it. In the coming years, of course, the avalanche of new media and new stars and reality show celebrities would finish the job of change that was started by men like Stamp and Caine and old London society would eventually be swamped in a tsunami of foreign wealth.

The mould was eventually broken and now it is hard to conceive how it could ever have seemed unusual for two men from ordinary backgrounds to rise to such heights of celebrity, but the world's nostalgic longing for what came before can be clearly seen in the viewing figures for *Downton Abbey* and royal weddings.

The reality of reality
television stars

"We've booked a suite at the Covent Garden Hotel," the publisher told me. "They're taking him straight there from the studios. He's contracted to stay in the room for a week and not talk to any other media. Stay with him till you have everything you need. We need the book by the end of the month."

I arrived at the hotel at the same moment as my new client, although it was hard to see him in the crowd of minders, producers, stylists, publicists, managers and everyone else plus their assistants that was milling around him, all hoping for a little of the stardust to rub off. At that moment he was the number one story in the tabloid media having just won the biggest reality show that week and, more importantly, having won the hearts of several hundred thousand teenage girls who might be accurately referred to as "our target market".

Reality television as we know it today started in the mid-nineties. There had been reality programmes before, such as *Candid Camera*, but the idea that the people who took part in the shows should become famous simply because they appeared on television screens was new. Some of the shows were linked to talent (*Opportunity Knocks, Stars in Their Eyes*, etc.), but increasingly they were based simply on whether the public liked the participants enough to want to watch them. If they wanted to watch them a lot then they would want to know more about them and there would then be other ways to merchandise both their looks and their personalities. One of the ways to do this was to write books about them or to get them to write books themselves. Most people lack the skills or experience needed to write books under that sort of pressure, and that is where we ghostwriters come in.

The young man at the centre of the storm in the hotel lobby looked happy but dazed and more than a little exhausted. Just a few weeks before he had been struggling his way through life at the bottom of the pile, much like everyone else, and now glossy, frothy magazine editors were offering him a quarter of a million pounds for a one day photo-shoot with a girl who was being swept along by the same reality television gravy train and they needed security whenever they were in public.

The publisher was allegedly shelling out similar money for the book — not to mention paying for a suite in one of the trendiest of celebrity hotels — then there were the music people wanting to get him into a studio and the rat pack of tabloid scandal-mongers and paparazzi scavenging around the lobby and in the street outside in search of any juicy scraps that might be chucked their way.

Once we were safely in the suite and the excitable young celebrity had worked out what a "concierge service" was and had put a good few things on the publishers' hotel bill, we started talking. It wasn't long before it was obvious that he was not going to be able to concentrate for long enough amidst the constant interruptions and distractions, each one more urgent than the last. We decided on a new plan. His mum would tell me the story of his life, while he bounced round the room and occasionally ventured out for fresh air, only to return a few minutes later flushed with the excitement of being chased by the media and fans, and often clutching a fresh newspaper or magazine bearing some entirely fictitious story about what he had been up to since the end of the show.

"I can't have done any of this," he would wail at us, partly amused, partly appalled, "I've been stuck in here with you."

Later, when the hardback book was in the shops and the publisher arranged a fanfare of publicity and interviews, an earnest journalist from one of the broadsheets asked him what it felt like to write a book.

"I didn't really," he said with the honesty which had so disarmed the show's viewers, "this posh bloke came to the hotel with a tape machine."

A few months later, when they were preparing to bring out the paperback, I went back for an update. By that stage the dust was settling on his overnight fame and he was living with his real girlfriend in a small one bedroom flat. Someone answered my insistent knocking at the door in what must have been their pyjamas.

"They're still in bed," I was told, "through there."

There were so many people sleeping or sitting around in the living room that it was easier just to close the bedroom door and climb into the warm bed with them, tape machine at the ready once more.

A genuine talent

Towards the end of the seventies I received a call from a publicity lady at the ICA, a small, artsy theatre venue in the Mall.

"We're putting on a play called *Talent* by a young writer called Victoria Wood and we wondered if you would like to interview her. You may have seen her singing funny songs on *New Faces* or *That's Life*. She's playing one of the lead roles as well. Believe me, she's going to be a huge star."

Publicists always tell you that people who aren't yet stars are going to be very soon, that's their job, but it was a free ticket and seemed like a good contact, so I happily went along.

Needless to say the play was a gentle revelation and although the young Miss Wood was painfully shy and modest she managed to be a joy to interview. Hearing or seeing someone who is genuinely honest and funny is always life-enhancing. Coming across French and Saunders in a fringe theatre somewhere, just before they broke through into television, I experienced the same rush of pleasure at seeing life from a different angle for the first time.

Playing back the interview with Victoria Wood afterwards, and then reading through her words once I had typed them up into an article for a women's magazine, I actually found myself laughing out loud again; a pretty fair indicator that the publicity lady's predictions were going to come true.

If Victoria Wood was the only thing that ever came out of the hundreds of thousands of hours of talent show television that the world has endured, it would still all have been worthwhile.

A real media circus

I had been invited to join a panel judging a literary prize. It was a serious opportunity for the writers who entered and had been created, like most literary prizes, to provide a publicity vehicle for the careers of those we judged the winners. Tired of meeting in offices and one another's houses, we decided to have our final judges' meeting in a traditional little French restaurant which happened, by coincidence, to be opposite the entrance to the hotel where I had spent a merry week with the reality show winner just a few months before.

Since one of our party was a regular at the restaurant we were given a table in the window. As the meal progressed and we debated the relative strengths of the competition entries, I noticed that people were gathering in the street outside the hotel.

As our discussion continued the crowd swelled and I saw that many of them knew each other and were carrying cameras. They were chatting amongst themselves with apparent casualness. Curious members of the public paused to see what was about to happen and it was beginning to be hard for the traffic to pass.

153

The moment Paris Hilton, the "It Girl" of the day, stepped out of the hotel entrance the relatively tranquil scene boiled up as the photographers elbowed one another and the tourists out the way, clambering over the bonnets and roofs of parked cars in their attempts to snatch their pictures.

A few hours later, as I made my way home through Victoria Station, I saw the star's face shining out from the front page of the evening paper. If only we could conjure up such feats of publicity for the young writers hoping that we were going to make them famous.

Culture clashes and other bad marriages

Human relationships lie at the heart of virtually all great stories. The more discordant the relationship the more fascinating it is for the reader and the more tightly it is likely to hold their attention, forcing them to keep turning the pages. Love stories have always been winners, and what happens when love dies is a close runner-up.

When people marry across class, racial and cultural barriers things hot up still further. From *Lady Chatterley's Lover* to *Guess Who's Coming to Dinner* and *Romeo and Juliet* the examples of great culture clashes are to be found everywhere in the literature of love.

Over the last 50 years, as multi-racial societies have proliferated and people have travelled further and more often than ever before, various patterns have emerged amongst the cross-cultural love stories that have filled the shelves of bookshops. Traditional tales of princesses falling in love with simple woodsmen and incurring the wrath of their parents have been replaced by more complex dilemmas.

First there were the women who wanted to talk about the agony of arranged or enforced marriages that had gone wrong, leading to terrible abuses and dramatic escapes. Then there were the women from Western cultures who found that dashing young Arabs and Iranians who had arrived in their cities on a wave of oil money and swept them off their feet, then led them into the heart of families who disapproved of everything they were and everything they did. There were tales of "mothers-in-law from hell", and "tugs of love" over children when each parent wanted to instil different cultural values into their offspring, some of them feeling so strongly that they were willing to actually kidnap them from their partners and sweep them off to other countries.

After the fall of the Berlin Wall hordes of beautiful and ambitious girls from the East marched to the West in search of jobs and rich husbands and it was the turn of Western men to fall in love and find themselves out of their depth culturally and emotionally, struggling to keep in touch with their children when their young wives disappeared back to their mothers, taking their children with them.

Sometimes the victims of these marital disasters would come to me hoping for a bestseller like Zana Muhsen's *Sold*, but many just wanted to have their side of the story set down so that when their children grew up they would be able to read how hard their estranged parents had fought to keep them. Better to discover that you were a victim of a "tug of love" than being left to believe that one of your parents simply didn't care enough to put up a fight.

Clubs for gentlemen and players

It is always best for ghosts to talk to their clients on the client's home territory. Whether that means a palace in Africa or a brothel in Bangkok, a château in the Dordogne or a stilted hut in the Malaysian jungle, it needs to be somewhere where they feel completely comfortable and safe enough to open their hearts and spill their secrets. They need, in other words, to feel able to "be themselves".

Sometimes fate intervenes. I had one client, for instance, who was forced to spend several hours a week in hospital on a kidney dialysis machine and managed to persuade the nursing staff on the ward that it would be a good use of her time if I and my tape machine sat at her bedside during those long tedious hours. It did, in fact, help to focus my mind on one of the main themes of the story, the effect that her health problems had had on her chances of fulfilling her dreams.

Sometimes it is not possible for the client to provide the venue, possibly because there would be no privacy at their home or because the writing of the book is a secret they are keeping from their family. Then neutral venues need to be found, places which offer the same safe environments plus plumbing and refreshments on demand. Hotels are often the best option. Bedrooms are good if it seems appropriate or meeting rooms if they are not too sterile. Often, however, it is the lobbies, lounges and restaurants that offer the best opportunities to sit in relative comfort, ordering cakes or alcohol when required, ignored by the floating population around you, most of whom are too busy with their own lives to bother listening in to the conversations of others.

If the client belongs to a club, that can serve in the same way. The grand gentlemen's clubs of Pall Mall make their grand members feel as safe as if they were in their own homes, surrounded by fleets of servants. Celebrities, particularly the younger ones, prefer the newer, flashier clubs, which tends to mean more interruptions as phones buzz and acquaintances come and go, kissing cheeks and exchanging snippets of news. Often in those situations there is also a minder/manager/publicity body in attendance, which is good if it makes the celebrity feel more comfortable and protected, bad if it makes them wary about baring their souls. These people are often paid to steer their clients away from saying anything that might be damaging to their image or might lead to a court case. It is almost impossible to make these guard dogs feel secure and their constant jumpiness often infects the clients, making them less willing to show their true selves, making them stick to the company line, making them talk as blandly as they would in a half hour magazine interview.

Modern recording devices make it far easier to hear what the storytellers are saying in loud, crowded places. Sometimes it is even clearer on the machine than it is face to face. It wasn't always so. In the days of cassette tapes I did an interview over lunch in the roar of the Savoy Grill and could hear nothing over the background noise, either during the lunch or afterwards in my office. Luckily, there were other opportunities to ask the same questions again later because the client had drunk so much claret at the lunch he was unable to remember anything we had spoken about.

A Year in Provence unleashes
an avalanche

In 1989 author and advertising man, Peter Mayle, published *A Year in Provence*, telling of his family's adventures while moving its home to the South of France in search of the "good life". It was by no means the first of the genre, as a child I was completely enthralled by Gerald Durrell's telling of his family's move to Corfu in *My Family and Other Animals*, but it was such an enormous bestseller amongst the book-chattering, Provence-loving classes that it launched an avalanche of imitators, some of which turned out to be much better than the original.

There were tales of people buying vineyards and opening restaurants, taking over stately homes and opening zoos and safari parks. Anecdotes about quaint locals, eccentric relatives and hilarious animals were mixed with recipes and travel stories. Publishers loved them and if the author had ever appeared on television and had a name that was recognisable to the public so much the better. Many of them needed the help of ghostwriters.

Visiting these people in their new and alternative lives was always entertaining. The sense of relief and joy that they conveyed at having been released from the tedium of their previous lives reminded me how lucky I was to be a freelance writer, the financial cliffs that they were often staring over made me shiver with recognition.

I always admired their courage. If I had followed a different path I don't know if I would ever have had the nerve to walk away from a secure life once I was used to a regular income, cushioned with a pension and paid holidays, in order to risk everything on being a writer. By starting at 17, when I had no debts, no dependants and outgoings that could be pared away to barest survival levels, sharing a flat with half a dozen or more other people, I had accidentally given myself a head start on the pursuit of the sort of "good life" that these escapees from the rat race were often searching for.

Jim Martin's island

Jim Martin had always cultivated an air of mystery, partly because he was naturally shy and partly because it added to his authority as an expert on the future of the planet and those of us who currently dwell on it. I think he would have rather enjoyed the idea that his death had a whisper of the Agatha Christie about it, his body found floating in the sea off his private island in Bermuda.

When I was first invited to meet Jim he was already a legend amongst those who were bringing Information Technology to the world. At the end of the eighties I was writing a company history for an IT consultancy that bore his name. Everyone had different stories to tell about him, some indisputably true, many more apocryphal. He had exotic homes around the world; he made millions of pounds a year from the books he had written about technology and from the lectures he gave. People like Bill Gates had gone to him for insights at the beginnings of their careers.

"Jim is thinking of writing an autobiography," the consultants told me, "will you meet him?"

Catching him on a flying visit between lectures, we met briefly and got on well. Socially awkward when it came to normal small talk, he became wildly enthused and animated when standing on stages or lecturing about all the subjects that caught his interest. I was very happy for him to talk constantly about the things that fascinated him. It was like receiving a crash degree course in technology at a time when I, like most of the world, still knew nothing of computers or the IT revolution that was about to change everything.

I went out to his house in Bermuda's Tucker's Town; it had two private beaches and a next door neighbour who had just run for the job of President of America. I stayed a week and Jim never stopped talking, never losing enthusiasm, never losing focus.

The book failed to find a publisher and we lost touch for a while, but I never forgot that week, or how much I had enjoyed the company of the tall, awkward, professorial Jim.

Some 20 years later he got back in touch to tell me he had just donated £100 million of his own money to Oxford University to found the Oxford Martin School of the 21st Century.

"And I've bought an island in Bermuda," he told me. "You and your wife must come out to stay. There is so much to talk about."

The invitation was irresistible. The island was magical and the result was a book called *James Martin: The Change Agent*, which was a mixture of biography and conversation, all set on the island.

We met several times after that at a variety of venues and he came to stay with us in England. He became a friend. I was shocked when reporters rang to tell me that his body had been found in the sea and to ask if I thought there might be foul play involved. I could also imagine how he would have turned the incident into another of the anecdotes that he polished and delivered so lovingly, both in lectures and in conversations. To be able to finish your life swimming around your own private island at the age of 80, when you started it as a working-class boy in war-torn England's Ashby de la Zouch, is no mean feat. I'd choose that every time over the option of a safe and sterile hospital bed, which was the answer I gave to the reporters.

Jim always said, "We can build any sort of world we want", which was just what he did.

A Russian in hiding

Ivan ventured out of hiding long enough for a meeting at a publisher's office in London. The editor was being exceptionally polite, even to the point of serving properly made coffee, which at the time was a rarity in any publisher's office. Ivan, I soon realised, was going to be investing heavily in the firm that had agreed to publish a series of novelised historical sagas based on his own family's history.

This was a year or two before the turn of the Millennium, when such deals were more generally called "vanity publishing" and the concept of "self-publishing" as an honourable pursuit was still a barely formed embryo in most people's minds. Everyone at the meeting, therefore, was choosing their words carefully. No one wanted to say anything that would upset Ivan's apparently sunny disposition because we had all heard that his explosions of temper could be as alarming as sudden electrical storms.

Ivan was a powerful, even overbearing character. He was enormously proud of the warrior status of his ancestors, many generations of whom had been pushed around various corners of the Soviet empire by

166

historical and political forces beyond their control. He had emerged from this difficult family history as a ferociously successful businessman and had made a considerable fortune after the fall of the Berlin Wall. He was very vague about the details but it had something to do with buying up state-owned industries. He was not a man who could be cajoled into talking about things that he didn't want to talk about. Several of his friends were behind bars in Russia and one of his closest friends had been assassinated.

I knew next to nothing about that part of the world and this seemed like a good way to find out a bit about its history from someone who had learned it from the stories his parents and grandparents had told, stories that had been handed down to them by previous generations.

Ivan had chosen Switzerland as his hiding place. He liked skiing so he had selected one of the oldest and grandest of ski resorts as his sanctuary from the world. He also liked to eat in five star restaurants and so he had bought a chalet within two minutes' walk of a legendary grand hotel. The hotel management provided him with housekeeping services within his chalet very like the ones they offered to their room guests, which meant he did not have to have any staff living in the house with him or interrupting his solitude unnecessarily. Ivan liked to keep his own company for as much of the day as was humanly possible.

He hired a room for me at the hotel and I would walk to the chalet each day so that we could talk, looking out from his living room over the pristine

Alpine view. At lunchtime we would go down to his garage. He would choose from the line of shiny four-wheel-drive monsters that he had collected there, and would drive us both to the underground car park at the hotel, a journey of no more than a hundred yards. We would then ascend to the dining room and sit by picture windows displaying the same Alpine view that we had just left. After lunch we would return to the chalet for another session. We would follow the same routine in the evening.

The tape machine would still be running on the table during the meals but Ivan's eyes were forever darting around the room and the family saga would often be interrupted by observations on other diners.

"That is the family of the Shah of Iran," he would whisper.

If anyone with an accent or the look of an Eastern European came into the room he would fall silent and hurry us through to the end of the meal so that we could purr back to the safety of the chalet. He was never clear about whom he feared was out to find him, but it was easy to imagine that he had made many enemies on his path to riches.

Education at Madame Jojo's

My middle daughter needed to make a film as part of her media studies A level and asked if I had any ideas. I was at the time working with the manager of an electro-pop act which had sold more than 20 million albums during the late eighties and nineties and I suggested that she should ask him if she could film an upcoming relaunch of the lead singer (who was also the manager's partner), as he was releasing a solo album.

The first venue for the relaunch was to be Madame Jojo's, an infamous nightclub in the heart of old Soho, which had become even more famous in the seventies when its owner, Paul Raymond, had turned it into a transvestite burlesque cabaret. Paul Raymond, like his Soho neighbour, Christina Foyle, had been one of the earliest London characters I had interviewed as a freelance journalist and I had retained an affectionate fascination for his seedy and glamorous little corner of the world ever since. There were rumours that by the time Raymond died his interests in Soho property had made him the richest man in England.

The pop singer's manager, an exceptionally kind man, liked the idea of having a student film crew adding to the buzz of the launch night, but one question still remained; would the school authorities, not to mention the parents of the film crew, be happy to have these vulnerable young minds let loose in one of the most infamously sleazy night joints in the history of the West End?

Fortunately my daughter had allies amongst the teachers and the project was given the green light. Partly in my role as parent/guardian and partly as a tourist from the seventies, I said that I would come too.

The star's name had worked its magic and the place was a heaving, sweating mass of bodies, almost exclusively male. The star himself was the sweatiest of all as he strutted his stuff on stage in a costume of leather and feathers. The students, enthralled at being allowed to step through a time warp into a real-life *Rocky Horror Picture Show*, behaved like professionals, moving with their cameras between the audience and dressing rooms with perfect discretion. I slid to the bar at the back of the room and found myself a stool from which to watch with a cocktail.

It had been a long time since I had been to a transvestite bar. The last time had been in Papeete, on a trip to Tahiti while I was still in my twenties. (My art teacher at school had whetted my appetite for the South Pacific when talking about Paul Gauguin's escape from civilisation to "paradise".)

I'd been working as a travel writer, a role that I was partly inspired to take on by Hugh Lofting's "Dr Dolittle" books. In my memory the doctor and his animal friends would spin a globe and the doctor would stab blindly at it with his finger. Whatever point his finger fell upon they would then set out to find. Maybe that only happened once in the whole series, but the image became immovably wedged in my mind and was, metaphorically speaking, pretty much how I chose the places I wanted to visit. Later, when I fell under the spell of Byron and his alter ego in *Childe Harold*, the image of the lone traveller took on an even more intense romance. The portly, balding fantasy figure of John Dolittle had grown into a world-weary, dissipated young Byronic hero — or so I hoped.

Hergé's adventures of Tintin also contributed to my urge to visit exotic foreign lands, his tales made all the more tempting by the fact that we were banned from reading them at prep school. The school authorities seemed to be under the impression that text mixed with pictures would be a hopelessly corrupting brew for our young minds, rendering us too idle ever to read solid blocks of text again. It's hard to imagine what those teachers would think of today's social media and entertainment mix, where everything comes in bite-sized pieces and usually in video or abbreviated text form.

I had lighted on the island of Tahiti while making my way from New Zealand to Hawaii, and had ended up staying in a gigantic resort hotel which seemed to cater almost solely for groups of pensioners getting on and off cruise liners. Even with the idyllic island scenery as a backdrop, this was not the paradise that I had imagined when daydreaming my way through art lectures a dozen years before.

Drowning my sorrows in a pool bar I got talking to a Finnish businessman who suggested we take a "*le truck*", the colourful and uncomfortable local mode of transport, into town. Wandering around town with my newly made friend we eventually ended the night in a transvestite bar. Lord Byron would undoubtedly have felt very at home lounging on those cushions, being entertained by the house cabaret, although I'm not at all sure what Dr Dolittle or Tintin would have made of it. By the next morning I had radically changed my view of the Finnish business community.

As the evening at Madame Jojo's wore on one of the teachers, who was youthful enough to look like he was part of the student team, wove his way over to me at the bar. He leaned close to be heard over the roar of the crowd and the throb of the speakers.

"Now this," he said, "is what I call education."

From the lips of an Iraqi child

It was the eleventh of September 2001. I would not normally be able to pinpoint the date of an interview so precisely without referring to a relevant diary, but this day would turn out to be memorable for everyone.

I was due to visit an English woman who was married to an Iraqi man and was telling the story of her life. Their home was north of Hyde Park, a part of London heavily populated by immigrants from Middle Eastern countries, their culture spilling out onto the streets from open-fronted shops and cafés in a heady mixture of scents and sounds and stacks of tempting, unfamiliar products. She and I were talking upstairs while her husband redecorated downstairs. To distract himself while he laboured he had the television on.

It was early afternoon and my client and I had been talking for three or four hours when her husband shouted urgently for us to come downstairs. When we got there we found him standing in front of the television, paintbrush in hand, staring at a cloud of smoke that was billowing from one of the twin towers of the World Trade Center.

173

The three of us stayed transfixed for an hour, trying to work out what was happening as the second aircraft hit the other tower and the commentators said there were other attacks expected.

The children needed picking up from their school round the corner and so my client's husband hurried off to collect them. When they returned the television was showing scenes of the buildings collapsing down onto the streets below, enveloping the city in an apocalyptic cloud of dust, smoke and debris.

"What's happening?" their eight-year-old asked, his eyes wide and serious.

"Someone is attacking America," their mother explained.

"Serves them right," the little boy shrugged, "after all the things they have done to us."

I love supermarket bookshelves

Supermarkets get a very bad press; blamed for killing the high street, for squeezing the profit margins of small suppliers, making us all obese . . . and so the list of accusations rolls on. But I confess I like the democratising effect they've had on many areas of life, including what they've done for bookselling. They only exist because we all secretly, and guiltily, like what they do for us. We show our approval by shopping there and all they do is give us more and more of what we want, when and where we want it.

The book trade has historically been one of the most vociferous of their critics, accusing the supermarkets of undercutting their prices and catering to the lowest common denominator. But I have to confess that were it not for the supermarkets many of the books I have been involved with, from celebrity autobiographies to misery memoirs, would never have seen the light of day. I'm sure there are many in the literary world who would think that was no bad thing, but I would contend that these books, which the more traditional booksellers never wanted to stock and publishers consequently didn't want to publish, are amongst the most accurate reflections available of our current times and our current obsessions.

If a time traveller arrived back at the beginning of the twenty-first century from some place far in the future, I would contend that he would learn more about the way most of us live from visiting a large supermarket than he would from visiting a bookshop or an art gallery or an opera house.

Supermarkets have created thousands of new book buyers who would never have stepped inside a traditional bookshop. (Many in the bookselling trade seem to be blissfully ignorant of just how intimidating bookshops can be to anyone who is unused to them.) They have brought pleasure to many tens of thousands of readers and opened the eyes of many thousands more to elements of life that were previously brushed under the carpet.

Led by the supermarkets, the traditional bookshops eventually started to stock the books that they had previously abhorred, even to the point of creating entire sections for them — or maybe ghettoes would be a better description.

By restricting the number of titles on offer the supermarkets made their shelves less intimidating to those who know and care little about the finer points of the literary world, and with clever merchandising and competitive pricing they made it easier for a customer to pick up a book and drop it into the trolley along with all their other purchases. Some would say that by doing so they "devalued" the book as an object, but I would suggest that by making it more accessible they increased the potential market for authors. The sort of books beloved of the more traditional readers will never make it onto the supermarket shelves and will be able to keep their prices higher for a little longer — but I am not sure that is necessarily a good thing. The people who decry the falling prices of books are often the same people who champion the provision of free books through libraries. It is hard to see why one source of cheap reading is a good thing while another is bad. I think books should be accessible to as many people as possible, both in terms of content and price and availability, which makes the supermarkets an ideal place to sell them.

With the arrival of Amazon and the self-publishing boom the supermarkets are no longer seen as the leading threat to the way things were. The trade always has to have someone to fear, someone to accuse of destroying what has gone before. Publishers mocked both *Oprah* in the States and *Richard & Judy* in the UK when they started their book clubs, until they realised that viewers of these shows could make or break some of their best authors.

I remember the independent bookshops complaining when Tim Waterstone first created his chain of bookstores at the beginning of the eighties, accusing him of trying to put them out of business. Many of the accusations they levelled against him were much the same as the ones they levelled at the supermarkets and then at Amazon. Now the Waterstones chain that once looked like Goliath to the smaller shops has come to resemble David in comparison to the new giants.

Reading an interview with Tim Waterstone I discovered that as a boy his first experience of book-buying was in a small retail outlet in the Sussex town of Crowborough, where I was born.

I was being taken to the same shop as a boy (about 15 years after him), and I don't think much can have changed in that time because my memories are almost identical to the ones he described to the journalist. Few provincial bookshops were good in those days, offering little choice and long waits if you ordered anything that wasn't already in stock. Things are a great deal better today and much of the improvement is due to the business models created by Tim Waterstone, the supermarkets and Amazon.

Confessions from the British Library

"You must have been here a hundred times," the young woman from the Society of Authors said as our guide ushered us up to the boardroom of the British Library for a privileged peek behind the scenes of one of the biggest municipal building projects ever undertaken in the world. Priceless literary treasures had been brought up and laid out for us to wonder at.

"Never been here before," I said, surprised to see how shocked she was by this confession.

"What, never?"

"No," I said, "honestly. It's never occurred to me."

"But what about research?"

"I think I must just write very superficial books."

She rejected this suggestion with all the politeness one would expect and when I later made the same confession to another member of the party, an extraordinarily distinguished biographer, he kindly pretended to be impressed that I had managed to write so many books without recourse to the many subterranean floors of material that lie beneath the building. There is close to 200 miles of shelving under the library's piazza, and almost the same again somewhere in Yorkshire. Was it arrogance that had led me to think I didn't need the help of these people in tracking down stories and following threads of truth? Was it idleness? Perhaps it was something else entirely.

Our guide took us out onto a balcony high above the floor of the reading room. The room had the proportions of a cathedral, the rows of desks filled with hundreds of readers and researchers poring silently over books and screens, lost in labyrinths of thought and information.

When persuading our son that he should go on to further education, even though he had no particular vocational path in mind, my wife and I had always glossed over the fact that neither of us had been to university, telling him that "not so many people did in those days". My wife tells me she regrets that she went straight from school to the world of work, but I have never regretted it for a second and that puzzles me because I love reading and I love thinking and I love writing, all of which should be available in spades during a university education.

Seeing behind the scenes of possibly the greatest library in the world was fascinating, but it still did not make me want to join the hordes on the reading room floor. It actually made me want to escape back into my own world and to go in search of a restaurant where I could maybe read a book over lunch, but more likely just watch the world go by and daydream.

Daydreaming was the thing I got into the most trouble for in school classrooms. It was my greatest pleasure but also my downfall, and has continued to fulfil both those roles ever since.

I think daydreaming finally gained the upper hand over educational endeavour when I was about 14 and from then on I found being confined to a classroom, or the effort of being forced to read a book which did not catch my imagination, almost intolerable, like a sort of mental suffocation. I had agreed to stay at school until I had at least taken some A levels and so I kept myself distracted by spending hours in the art room and the drama department. Being able to draw and paint pictures, perform and create scenery absorbed me because they allowed my mind to wander most of the time.

I started tapping away at my first novel when I was 15 and I was writing sketches for school reviews as well as appearing in them. Most of the time during those years, however, I sat around for hours on end smoking cheap cigarettes, talking nonsense, listening to music on portable record players and staring into space. I was waiting impatiently for the moment when the whole ordeal would be over and I could take full control of my life and head for London and on from there into the rest of the world.

I was breathlessly reading *Room at the Top*, *Of Human Bondage* and *Keep the Aspidistra Flying*, listening to Johnny Cash singing about his "Folsom Prison Blues" and watching *If*, Lindsay Anderson's film about a rebellion in a public school remarkably like the one I was incarcerated in, as I tried to work out what the coming years were going to be like. The thought of going on to spend three more years in an institution where I might not be able to daydream as much as I wanted was not attractive.

The liberating effect of Lindsay Anderson's film had been the direct opposite of *Tom Brown's Schooldays*, which I misguidedly read before embarking on my senior school and which gave me every expectation of being "roasted" over an open fire by sadistic prefects. Another Victorian novel, *Vice Versa*, did little to calm my fears of what fate lay in store for me, nor the later adventures of Billy Bunter at Greyfriars School.

The relatively liberal atmosphere which I actually found myself in when I arrived at Lancing at the age of 13, overseen by Sir William Gladstone, a wise and benevolent headmaster and great grandson of the Victorian Prime Minister, gave me hope that life might just improve as I moved closer to the end of the long, tedious years of childhood and formal education.

By the time the envelope containing my final pitiful exam results arrived at my parents' house I was already renting a room in a shared flat in Earls Court, ruled over by a flamboyant resting actor, and was starting the long struggle to support myself from my writing. Never for a second was I tempted back into any classroom until people started inviting me to be the one on the podium doing the talking.

"You may just have to get a job..."

"So, young man, what do you plan to do with your life?"

It's one of the most annoying questions that well-meaning people ask of the young as soon as they leave school or university, and at most points before and in between.

It may be annoying, but even the most innocent, or rebellious, of young people know that finding the answer is the key to everything. When you get to the other end of your working life and look back, these people are asking, what sort of path do you want to see stretching out behind you?

In some ways I was one of the fortunate ones. From the age of 16 I had an almost clear idea of what I wanted that path to look like, but when I described it out loud it sounded pretty naive, not to mention vain, so I tended to respond to interrogation by looking down and mumbling something non-committal like everyone else.

What I knew I wanted was to be free to follow anything that caught my interest. I wanted to attack life like an overexcited dog hurtling back and forth along a ripe hedgerow, chasing every tempting scent and every promising rustle of leaves. I wanted to have learned as much as possible about as wide a variety of subjects as possible. I wanted to be in a position to take advantage of any unexpected opportunities that might be offered to me. I wanted to be able to make my own decisions as to how I planned my life and spent my days. I wanted to surrender my fate to serendipity while at the same time being able to make enough of a living to support myself and whatever family might come along (something else that would be in the hands of the God of Serendipity). I wanted to get to the end of the path with as many good and varied memories and stories as possible — and, of course, I wanted to meet girls, as many as possible.

The thing I was most frightened of, along with possible starvation, was boredom. If I couldn't continually distract and stimulate myself with thoughts and adventures that interested me I knew I would be in danger of sliding into the shadows of despondency, and hurtling on down from there into the pit of despair.

There appeared to be a few options that fitted these criteria; the three front runners were writing, art and acting, all of which seemed to provide the necessary highs needed to stay ahead of the black cloud of depression, but at the same time they offered the constant threat of rejection. It required a fair degree of blind, and naive, optimism to commit to any of these paths. If I voiced my ambitions out loud I ran the risk of hearing other people's opinions on just how likely it was that I would starve to death if I tried to make any of them my life, so on most occasions I would decide it was better to keep my own counsel.

My first year in London had not gone that brilliantly financially. As well as writing anything and everything I could think of, and selling none of it, I had also dipped my toe into the acting world, which basically meant being a background extra for the odd day's filming (including an appearance as a footman in a powdered wig in a filmed history of prostitution, my task being to literally "serve up" Cora Pearl, a famous nineteenth-century courtesan, on a platter to Edward VII while he was the Prince of Wales), and getting the occasional photographic modelling job.

These scraps of employment had paid the £7.50 a week rent on my room in the shared flat in Earls Court and not much else. It was fun but it was increasingly difficult to fool anyone that I was ever going to be able to support myself on this path.

"You may just have to get a job."

My father's perfectly sensible words sent a chill of horror rippling through me. The words he didn't say, but which seemed to hang in the air between us were, "like everyone else."

We were meeting for supper in London, as we sometimes did when he thought I needed feeding, and were having a drink in the bar at the top of the Park Lane Hilton, which was then the highest building in the area, so that we could both gaze out over the city lights during any lulls that might fall in the conversation. He liked taking me to places like that and mostly I enjoyed these peeks into the life he led on his company expense account when he wasn't at home with my mother. Even going with him for a drink at the Playboy Club was an interesting, if somewhat disquieting, experience. I knew several girls who worked as bunnies and was all too familiar with what their real views were of the club members they were trained to serve with such bright smiles.

Taking horrified offence at his suggestion that I should get a job like everyone else, but making a huge effort to hide it, I vowed to myself that I would demonstrate my disdain by getting the most obviously boring job going, the sort of thing that George Orwell, Somerset Maugham, Evelyn Waugh, Graham Greene and my other influences would have held up as an example of the sort of living death that any young creative soul should avoid at all costs. Then, I told myself, my father would see the error of his thinking and would be sorry he had crushed my great creative potential.

My father, probably assuming that he had just given me a sound piece of paternal advice, was by then studying the menu, apparently unaware of the turmoil his words had caused inside his son's head.

The following day I resigned myself to the fact that I was now officially a failed actor/writer/artist and set about job-hunting with a heavy, angry heart. I bought an *Evening Standard* and secured some interviews. It seemed a good idea to exaggerate a little to these potential employers as to the A level results I had achieved. My former headmaster gave me a generous reference, accompanied by a kind letter assuring me that this change in direction might prove more rewarding than I was fearing. I was grateful for this attempt at consolation, but remained convinced he was mistaken.

I was offered three different jobs, but only one of my interviewers failed to ask to see any evidence of the exam results I was claiming. That was the job I, therefore, had to accept. Thus, within a frighteningly short time, I found myself a shipping clerk for the United Africa Company in an office in Blackfriars, spending my days filing bills of lading and my evenings in the company's amateur dramatics club. I was 18 years old and it felt in the darkest hours of the night as if my life was at an end already. There seemed nothing to do but hope for some sort of miracle.

Within a few months I realised that no miracle was coming and no one was ever going to notice that this was a gesture of defiance and not simply a sensible career move. I had backed myself into a corner and was now lost in an office which held little potential for anyone wanting eventually to earn a living as a writer. Rather than realising that they had caused me to ruin my life, my parents actually seemed fairly relieved that I was now earning a steady salary. It dawned on me that if I didn't want to spend my life filing bills of lading I was going to have to do something about it myself.

To quote the blurb on the back cover of my battered Penguin edition of *Keep the Aspidistra Flying*, the story of Gordon Comstock who saw the aspidistra as the symbol of the artist selling out to the comforts and security of dull, middle-class respectability: "in his mulish determination to embrace the full agony of poverty, he walked out of one 'good' job after another, to the despair of his friends. For him the Embankment was nobler than the aspidistra, symbol of spiritual death." I think that was pretty much what was going on in my head, although I lacked even Comstock's courage because I intended to do all I could to avoid ending up sleeping on the Embankment.

In my desperation to escape this self-triggered trap, I contacted everyone I had met in my first year in London, begging for any possible ways out and, to my amazement, gordon eden-wheen (he insisted on no capital letters, such were the pretensions of the time), an agent who had got me a couple of modelling jobs the previous year, asked if I would like to be his assistant since he had to be out of the office a lot producing fashion shows during "the season".

Run a modelling agency? Did I have to think for even a second before accepting?

The money was about half whatever I was earning as a shipping clerk, but the decision still seemed like an absolute no-brainer since one of my most urgent priorities since leaving my single-sex school was to meet as many young women as possible in as short a time as possible. Had there ever been a place more tailor-made for providing such opportunities in abundance?

Soon after I took up the new job, based in a room off a photographer's studio in Charlotte Street, eden-wheen was invited to merge his agency with a large modelling school in the middle of Bond Street, providing me with still more chances to meet young women and at the same time opening up any number of opportunities for finding material to write about.

Within a year I was back on course towards being a full-time freelance writer, mainly selling my services for public relations purposes, with the modelling school as one of my clients. Public relations was still a fledgling industry, which is the only explanation I can give as to how a 20-year-old with virtually no experience was able to make a living from it. I even used to lecture on the subject for the modelling school's rivals, Lucie Clayton, a secretarial and finishing school that had become famous in the sixties for producing the most glamorous models of the day, although I can't for a moment imagine that I had any wisdom worth listening to.

By this stage I had decided that being a writer really was the only way I could see that I could ensure a satisfactory level of personal freedom and variety, and hopefully earn a living. But what should I write about? There were plenty of interesting stories and people to choose from but I couldn't see how to turn them into a living wage.

I tried every possible road that a writer can take and there were many times when it seemed impossible that I would ever be able to earn a steady living from such a precarious profession. To public relations I added business writing and then travel writing, and in every spare moment I was trying to write books. I only ever took two full-time jobs after that, one in a public relations consultancy and the other on a media trade magazine. Neither job lasted more than a few months and I eventually had to admit that I was probably never going to be capable of holding down any permanent position. I was now set irrevocably on a course where self-employment was the only option. Had I realised quite how choppy the waters I was sailing into would turn out to be I don't know if I would have had the courage to do it ... Who am I kidding? I had no option.

The forgotten rules of grammar

As a result of my lamentable inability to concentrate in school classrooms, I do not have any grasp of the rules of grammar. I must have known some of them once because I got English, Latin and French O levels, I think, but they no longer reside in my memory. I rely entirely on whether something "sounds" right (by which I also mean "reads" right), like a musician who can't read music and is forced to play by ear.

If it doesn't sound right then I am able to put it right but I am not able to find any of the technical terms needed to describe most of the types of words or grammatical constructions that I have used. I can identify nouns, verbs, adjectives and adverbs, and I might be able to name a few tenses, but after that I have to resort to the dictionary every time someone mistakes me for an expert and asks me what a subjunctive or a subordinate clause might be. I can only identify a split infinitive because of *Star Trek*'s "to boldly go" catchphrase.

I write and read as instinctively as I talk, with none of the scaffolding of knowledge that I would probably need if I were ever to be asked to teach creative writing.

Those instincts, I believe, came from being talked to like an adult from as early as I can remember (I was an only child and my mother did not find childish talk interesting), being read to and being given well-written books to read so that their written language seeped into my head as surreptitiously as spoken languages seep into the mouth of every infant.

My mother tempted me into reading for myself by agreeing to read alternate chapters of *A Bear Called Paddington* to me as long as I read the others for myself. The urge to follow the polite bear's adventures was enough to get me hooked and soon I was making my own way, reading everything I could find in the local library and on my mother's bookshelves — which meant I had read virtually every one of Georgette Heyer's regency romances by the time I was 12 and was deep into saving foppish aristocrats from the guillotine with the Scarlet Pimpernel.

I use language much as a well-trained gun-dog might use his nose and ears. When it works well it is a triumph of habit and practice and nothing to do with intellectual rigour, powers of deconstruction or analysis.

I never managed to learn my multiplication tables either, but at least I'm not trying to earn my living as a mathematician.

A forgotten weekend in academia

"We once spent a weekend together," I said as I reintroduced myself to the country's oldest and most distinguished crime writer at a party deep in Mayfair.

"Did we?" she asked, smiling sweetly but looking entirely blank.

"In Cambridge," I prompted, "King's College."

"What on earth were we doing there?" she asked with what sounded like genuine amazement.

It was a good question. I think she and I were the only working writers around the mighty conference table. Everyone else appeared to be either an academic or a lawyer. I believe we had been invited to discuss something to do with the legal implications of writing about living people, but like her I am more than a little hazy as to why that was deemed to be a good way for anyone to spend a weekend.

I remember there was a sumptuous dinner involved, evoking scenes from Tom Sharpe's university satire, *Porterhouse Blue*, put before us by discreet college servants who would not have looked out of place serving Lord Byron. I also remember extremely spartan bedrooms, which would not have looked out of place in a Victorian prep school.

One of the most curious things about growing older is that some incidents from your past begin to take on the appearance of dreams or half-forgotten movies.

A little lone wolf

"The eagle is probably the most powerful bird in the world, always flying alone, never in a crowd." The Middle Eastern merchant prince was talking with his eyes shut, a habit which, when coupled with long pauses, sometimes made it hard to tell if he had fallen asleep mid-thought.

My tape machine was taking care of preserving his widely spaced words, his closed eyes giving me the opportunity to look around the Aladdin's cave of a room. Every inch of the mighty floor space was filled with objects elaborately decorated in gold. Anything that wasn't gold was white or cream, from the endless sofas and the cushions of the heavily gilded thrones that we were sitting in to the tissue boxes that were carefully placed in order to be constantly within reach of anyone wishing to expectorate unexpectedly.

Around us were panoramic views of Hyde Park from the windows of one of the apartments in the newly built Knightsbridge block that was reported to contain the most expensive homes in London.

As a child I had often visited the site in its previous incarnation as Bowater House since it had contained my father's office. Bowater House was one of the ugliest modern office blocks to go up in London after the Second World War. There has been a story told that in 1959 Ludwig Mies van der Rohe, the pre-eminent master of modern architecture, was taken past Bowater House in a taxi. His companion, Ernö Goldfinger, another eminent architect and designer, motioned towards the building.

"This is all your fault," Goldfinger said.

"I was not," Mies van der Rohe replied icily, "the architect of that building."

Anyway, the building was demolished in 2006 and replaced with this equally controversial structure which seems to many to typify the dangerous gap that is opening up between the global super-rich and the rest of us in the twenty-first century.

"Birds that move around in flocks make easy targets for any lone predator," my client resumed his musings without lifting his eyelids. "If you move in crowds you often end up being punished for the sins of others."

He fell silent again, his eyelids still lowered and I pondered his words. I remembered an afternoon soon after starting at my first boarding school. I was seven years old and walking on my own in the grounds in one of the few moments of the day that was not crammed full of sport, lessons and pointless regimentation. One of my school reports of the time, which my wife sweetly unearthed from the cellar recently to amuse the children, claims that, "Andrew believes his contemporaries offer limited intellectual stimulation — he is not always an easy person to deal with but one that is learning to be more tolerant", which could explain why I was walking on my own, at several levels.

Rounding a corner I bumped into a teacher on routine patrol duty.

"Why aren't you with friends, Crofts?" she asked in a voice that was not without a hint of kindness. "You're a funny little lone wolf, aren't you?"

I prefer my client's analogy of the lone eagle soaring proudly across open skies.

The greatest living playwright

There was always an extra buzz of excitement at the Biographers' Club Christmas party when one of the club's grandest lady biographers brought her husband along. He was a man widely seen at the time as Britain's greatest living playwright, the closest thing you would find to a "household name" in the cultural world.

Moving, as one does at these sorts of parties, from one conversational group to another, I found myself next to the grand lady biographer after the wine had been flowing for a while. She made the usual polite enquiry as to what I did for a living (coincidentally her equally splendid mother and father had been two of the literary grandees who had made similar polite enquiries at the first Foyles Literary Lunch I attended nearly 40 years before. Then I would have told them I was a novelist or perhaps a journalist).

When I explained that I ghosted books and that many of them were memoirs she loudly summoned her husband to join us from another nearby group.

"You need to talk to this man," she instructed him. "He's a ghostwriter. You've been saying for years that you are going to write about your wartime evacuee experiences and you're never going to get round to it. Why don't you just let him do it?"

For just a moment it looked as if the greatest living playwright was actually weighing up the benefits of having someone else lift the burden of authorship from his shoulders, but the moment passed and the polite conversations rolled on. He died a year or two later and I suspect he never got round to writing down those memories, although his wife wrote a moving, and bestselling, account of their relationship.

The selling power of celebrities

Alexandre Dumas, père, had a ghostwriter, or "nègre" as folks like me are sweetly referred to over in France. His name was Auguste Jules Maquet. In the 1830s Maquet, a novelist and playwright, had tried to have one of his own works published but was told: "You have written a masterpiece, but you're not a name and we only want names."

Nothing has changed apart from the scale of this hunt for "names". Marketing books is one of the hardest tasks any business person can take on and anything which makes the titles more noticeable to the public is going to be irresistible. Celebrities are consequently created and nurtured specifically for the purpose of selling products from movies to perfume, clothes to books. If an author is not a celebrity then the publisher will do their damnedest to make them one — usually with limited success.

A diet book by a film star is certain to gain more column inches than one written by an unknown doctor, a memoir by a television soap star is far more likely to get a six figure deal than one by a distinguished Shakespearian stage actor who appears nightly in front of audiences numbered in their hundreds rather than their millions.

Realising how useful it is to have a cast of characters who are known to wide segments of their markets, business people who want to attract the attention of customers need to invent celebrities to do the talking for them. To begin with these celebrities were people who had genuinely achieved something remarkable or unusual, like winning a war or being crowned king. Then they began to be drawn from the entertainment and acting worlds. Eventually that supply also proved inadequate for the marketing needs of the modern world. The newspapers were able to invent some of their own by inflating and personalising scandals and court cases, but it was the proliferation of the television and music industries that was to provide the most fruitful opportunities for creating celebrities that other people would want to listen to or watch.

Many of these people end up wanting to write books or are asked to put their names to books in order to help sales, and so they find themselves sitting down with people like me.

The most surprising thing is how very "normal" many of them are. They might have been involved in "news" stories that have kept them on the front pages for weeks on end. They might star in television programmes which are watched by tens of millions, but more often than not they live very ordinary lives in very ordinary houses with very ordinary partners and fret about all the same things as everyone else.

Most have virtually no power over their own destinies. The ones who appear in the television programmes are generally treated like commodities by their producers and masters, who pay them little or nothing, work them like slaves and decide when they are going to be killed off by scriptwriters or reality television judges. The ones that the media decides to love never know when the editors are going to turn on them, withdrawing the airbrushing services that made them look so desirable in early photographs and pointing out their cellulite on the beach at the same time as exposing their private lives to ridicule.

It is certainly true that these celebrities put themselves up for fame by auditioning and giving interviews and frequenting the places where the paparazzi will find them easily, but most of them have little or no conception of what they are letting themselves in for when they set out on this road as bright-eyed young hopefuls. The clever ones exploit the system (step forward Victoria Beckham and Katie Price as the most fabulous modern-day examples), but most are no match for the business and media manipulators who make them and break them at will.

Simply being famous is never going to be enough to make an interesting book. There must be another story going on unless it is going to be a picture book for fans, like the titles that hit the shelves within a week of a boy group winning, or maybe losing, the final of *The X Factor*. In those cases the book is no more than a memento of the moment, like a very thick fan magazine or concert programme. It is all part of the merchandising campaign and intended to be ephemeral. In some cases the producers have manuscripts prepared for all the finalists in the last weeks of a competition so that they are ready to start printing the winner's story, and any others that the publisher believes to be sufficiently commercial, the moment the results are known.

To create a full-length book which people will actually read, however, the ghostwriter has to find another, deeper story. It might be overcoming a difficult illness, an abused childhood or an abusive relationship, a controversial court case or a high profile divorce, a drug habit or a criminal record — anything that adds another level to the story. Merely appearing in a programme in front of millions of people may well get you into a meeting with a publisher but it won't necessarily get the public to shell out their hard-earned cash or tempt them to devote the time needed to reading it.

A highly regarded literary novelist of my acquaintance was once commissioned to ghostwrite the autobiography of one of the stars of *EastEnders*, only to find that she had no real back story at all.

"There is a limit," he sighed over a large glass of wine, "to how many different ways you can describe the sound of Bow Bells."

If a celebrity has a long career of genuine achievement, of course, and has been particularly skilful at keeping their private life private, managing to retain an air of mystery (as with stars like the Beatles, the Rolling Stones and David Bowie), then there may still be enough of an appetite amongst the general public for more information to make a book a bestseller, as Keith Richards demonstrated when he finally wrote his autobiography *Life* with ghostwriter James Fox (the author of *White Mischief*). In 2013 Morrissey and Penguin were very successful at managing to pique the interest of fans as to what new things their idol might still have left to say.

Haters of the celebrity world are always quick to point out when sales of celebrity books dip, but the truth is that whenever someone famous who is also interesting steps forward with something new to say, whether they are a bad-tempered football manager or an allegedly drug-soaked rock star, then large numbers of people will always pay to read the result.

The soap star who came to stay

It was her mother who made the call, struggling not to cry. "He's been round again, Andrew," she said, "and he's made a right mess of her this time. She's terrified he's going to come back."

She didn't have to tell me who it was she was talking about. Her daughter was a current hot property in a soap opera, much loved by the tabloids that hounded her constantly for stories about her private life, which was why the publisher had been willing to buy her autobiography. Her biggest problem was an ex-boyfriend who liked to foster an image of himself as a gangster and all-round hard-man. The couple had a child together and she had gone on to have another with her current boyfriend. The ex-boyfriend didn't like the idea of his child being brought up by another man and had taken to coming round and threatening her. The threats sometimes became reality. Once or twice the tabloids had commented on black eyes that she had not managed to cover up in front of their photographers, but this time it sounded like he had gone further.

"I don't know how to ask this," her mum went on, "but she needs somewhere safe to go for a few days.

She can't come to me because he knows where I live. Could she and the kids come and stay with you for a few days while she works out what to do?"

"Sure," I heard myself say.

My wife took the news pretty well. Our biggest worry was how our children would react to seeing their first badly beaten woman, but that didn't seem like a good enough reason to turn away someone who appeared at that moment to have no one else to turn to. What her mum had forgotten to mention was that the current boyfriend would also be coming, as would their hyperactive dog. Our children adjusted very quickly to the new family in our midst, enjoying looking after younger children, but our Labrador had something close to a nervous breakdown at having her home space so boisterously invaded.

After a few days of countryside peace and calm our heroine was refreshed and ready to return to the fray, bravely facing down the lenses of the paparazzi and the threats of the ex-boyfriend. Our children returned to their normal, safe, predictable routines with a lot to think about and the Labrador was able to sleep with both eyes shut once more. I'm not sure which family benefited the most from the experience.

Not everyone can be Hamlet

If there is one skill needed to succeed in life it must be the ability never to allow disappointment or rejection to stop you from trying again. Everyone has to face those twin demons from time to time, but if you choose to follow a profession like writing then you are going to be coming up against them most days.

To find the energy and patience to write a full-length book you have to believe in it wholeheartedly, you must be filled with optimism and enthusiasm, despite the fact that everyone knows the odds against any book being a success, or even finding a publisher and an audience, are enormous. The more you love the story and the more time you dedicate to perfecting it, the more disappointed you are likely to feel if it is rejected. You know you shouldn't take the rejection personally, but inevitably you do. Each rejection takes another small bite out of your soul; wounds which even the greatest triumphs will never quite heal.

In my last two years at school I was fortunate to have a tutor, Dave Horlock, who was only 10 years older than me, although 26 seemed enormously ancient to me at the time. He became famous within the school for producing spectacular school plays to what seemed to us to be almost professional standards. He became a friend as well as a tutor, introducing me to the wonders of Oscar Wilde (I was already spending much of my time doing imitation Aubrey Beardsley posters in the art room, so it wasn't a hard sell) and Lord Byron, and tasking me first with the creation of the sets and scenery for his productions and then giving me acting roles after seeing me perform as a bored "Bottom" in a classroom dramatisation of *A Midsummer Night's Dream*.

He helped me pass many long evenings in conversation when I probably should have been working for my exams, having escaped across the quadrangle from my study and climbed the stone spiral staircase to his rooms in the turret of one of the Gormenghast-like towers, collapsing onto the sofa with his dog.

There must have been something in the sea air that swirled around those towers and quadrangles, which encouraged daydreamers to try writing. Evelyn Waugh was there during the First World War (and published *Decline and Fall*, a deadly satire of the teaching world, when he was 25). Jan Morris was there at the end of the thirties (although known as James Morris then), and went on to become one of the world's greatest travel writers. Tom Sharpe arrived there around 1940 and become famous for his comedic novels, particularly the university-based *Porterhouse Blue*. Sir Tim Rice, the lyricist, arrived in the mid-fifties, followed by the playwright David Hare around 1960, who has written about his time there in a play called *South Downs*. Fellow playwright and screenwriter, Christopher Hampton, would have been there at much the same time as Hare.

The first I knew that Dave Horlock had other plans than being a school teacher all his life was when he announced that he was leaving at the end of term in order to become a professional director at a well-known provincial theatre company. I was devastated to lose a friend who had made the long school evenings interesting, particularly as I had been looking forward to doing one more production with him before I too left. He admitted that his only regret about leaving so suddenly was that he wouldn't be able to stage the play that he had been planning.

"What were you planning?" I asked.

"*Hamlet*," he replied. "I was going to ask you to play the lead."

"You were going to ask me to play Hamlet?"

A tidal wave of disappointment swept away any possible pride or excitement at the thought that he had been going to offer me such an opportunity. A near miss, after all, is as good as a failure, and there are always going to be more near misses in life than there are going to be bullseyes. Over the following years I would experience that same feeling many times whenever an agent would fail to ring back when promised or an editor who had raved about a manuscript had to break the news that they couldn't persuade anyone in their sales team to share their enthusiasm, or a book which I was certain the public would love sank without a trace within weeks of publication.

For most writers, just like actors and artists, it takes us many years before we can support ourselves from our chosen craft, and even once we are established we continue to be hit by disappointments and rejections more often than not. Most people find the odds too daunting and fall by the wayside as the years go by. Those who succeed are the ones who just keep going, refusing to give up, always trying new ideas, always creating new material, always believing that there is no other way to live.

There will always be shooting stars, people who hit lucky first time and soar much higher and faster than everyone else. They are the people who get written about in the media most often, but the reason they get into the media is because they are unusual. Those moments of good luck, or divine inspiration, will happen to nearly everyone eventually, if they just keep going. "Every dog," as the saying goes, "has its day." And if they never happen? Well, you will still have had an interesting time chasing them along the way.

Discovering Jay Gatsby

"Have you read this?" my tutor asked, lobbing a copy of *The Great Gatsby* into my lap.

I started it that night and didn't bother to go to any lessons the next day because I wanted to finish it and then spend time thinking about the knot of excitement that it had left in my stomach.

This, I decided, was who I wanted to be — Jay Gatsby. There was the immense personal fortune, the mysterious past, the magnificent parties, the mansion, the wardrobe full of pink suits — who could ask for anything more?

It is not surprising I was so transfixed, because it was exactly the sort of effect F. Scott Fitzgerald had wanted to achieve. "So he invented," he wrote of Gatsby, "just the sort of Jay Gatsby that a 17-year-old boy would be likely to invent, and to this conception he was faithful to the end."

Although I was deeply attracted to the idea of getting inside the lives of people like Gatsby, I also wanted to be sure I could walk away before things turned nasty. After a while it dawned on me that it was the narrator, Nick Carraway, that I really wanted to be. He was a writer staying in a cottage in the grounds of the mansion. He became involved with the dissolute lives of the main characters, uncovered the very stuff of their souls and then went back to the solitary safety of his home to write his story once things got dangerous.

"I was within and without," Carraway wrote, "simultaneously enchanted and repelled by the inexhaustible variety of life."

That, I decided, was what being a writer would be like.

"The Principessa is throwing a party..."

"What is happening on the beach?" my mother enquired of the waiter as we watched troops of formally uniformed staff carrying chairs down from where we were sitting with pre-dinner drinks on the terrace.

"The Principessa is throwing a party," the waiter replied, assuming that the activity required no more explanation than that.

He was right. Tom, my best friend, who had been invited to join us so that my parents didn't have to bear the full weight of my company throughout the holiday, and I were well aware of the Principessa and her entourage since arriving at the Tunisian beach resort. We must have been about 12 years old; an age when we found it hard not to gawp at a beautiful Italian princess as she glided around the complex in Jackie Kennedy sunglasses, apparently oblivious of our fascination.

We ate dinner faster than usual as the sun set across the horizon, eager to get down to the beach and watch the revellers from a better vantage point, anxious that we might miss something.

Long tables had been set out beneath the undulating canopies and the uniformed hotel staff were moving back and forth between the semi-naked guests and the various meats which were turning over open fires. There was a babble of languages, none of which we understood, and music we had never heard before. Flaming torches took over from the sunset as we crouched on the sand outside the flickering light, drinking in every detail of the illuminated scene, inventing our own back stories for every guest there. It was my first modest glimpse of the international jet set (a new concept at the time) at play. It seemed richer and more glamorous than any film I had ever seen. We sat there for hours, intoxicated by the scent of smoke and jasmine and the possibilities of what adult life might hold in store.

A black BMW behind
King's Cross

"Remind me again who you're going to see today," my wife said, looking up from the family breakfast table as I prepared to leave for the station. These were the days before everyone automatically carried a phone around with them all day. Once I left the house we probably wouldn't speak again until I got home that evening.

"I'm not sure," I admitted.

"What do you mean, you're not sure?"

"Some chap who wants to write a novel about the secret world of bodyguards and mercenaries. I think he works for one of the Middle Eastern royal families."

"Cool," my son said through a mouthful of Rice Krispies. "Will he have a gun?"

"Where are you meeting him?" My wife now looked alarmed.

"Behind King's Cross."

"Where behind King's Cross?"

"I'm not sure," I said, realising that I was sounding evasive. "He said he would meet me there, behind the station."

"But how will you know him?"

"He's going to be in a black BMW."

"Don't get killed, will you, Daddy," one of the girls piped up cheerfully.

"Just a minute . . ." Her interrogatory glare was unnerving me. "Are you telling me that if you don't come home tonight and I have to ring the police . . ." I cast a quick glance at the children, all of whose eyes were now boring into me, "and they ask me where you were going today, I have to tell them that all I know is you were meeting a man in a black BMW behind King's Cross?"

"Well, when you put it like that . . ." I tried an ironic little chuckle in the hope that it would put things back into perspective and stop the youngest girl's bottom lip quivering so ominously. "I can leave you the number that he called from if that would put your mind at rest."

Needless to say the mystery man turned out to be perfectly amiable and had put together a pretty good plotline which needed to be turned into a full-scale manuscript, but I made a note to self that day that responsible husbands and fathers have to be a little more careful not to alarm their families through sheer carelessness.

Tales of courtesans and mistresses

"You got a call while you were out," my wife said as I came in the door, studiously staring at the vegetables, which she was cutting up for supper with more vigour than strictly necessary.

There was a tension in the air and my usually ineffective male antenna was warning me to tread carefully.

I had informed her as I left that morning that I had a meeting in London with a woman who was at the time infamous for her exploits as a courtesan amongst the highest and mightiest in the land. The woman had been seamlessly professional at the meeting with the publisher and the old boy had fallen in love just as heavily as she had intended. After the meeting she and I had repaired to the bar at the Dorchester for a celebratory drink. The outfit she had chosen for maximum impact at the meeting was so tightly fitted to her figure, and so lacking in any excess material, that she had not had anywhere to store any cash. She protested her embarrassment at finding herself unable to pay for the drink she wanted to buy me, but I was quite happy to fork out since her eyelash-fluttering performance had definitely added another zero to the publisher's offer. Now I was trying to divine why my wife might be avoiding eye contact so obviously.

"Oh yes?" I said. "Who was that?"

"She said she didn't need to leave a name because you would know who it was. She had a foreign accent; all very breathy." Still her eyes were fixed on the execution of the innocent vegetables giving up their lives to the blows from her knife. "She said to tell you 'thank you'."

"That's it?"

"That's it. Although actually it sounded more like 'tank you'."

Those who have had affairs with people of importance, either paid or not paid, often seem to feel the need to vent their frustrations in print when things go pear-shaped. Sometimes it is because they need the money; sometimes it is for the sheer mischief-making hell of it. Sometimes they have even been married to the person of importance and want to vent the spleen which their divorce has built up in them, usually aided by their legal teams. Mostly they don't have stories that the publishers, or indeed the public, feel they want to pay money for, but now and then one will catch the public's imagination. The soldier who wrote about his affair with Princess Diana was probably the most successful in this genre, but there have been others.

Those who make a living in this manner have various ways of introducing themselves when they first make contact with a ghost. Some like to come straight out with the announcement that they are "high class prostitutes" (in reality the "low class" ones often have the more interesting stories to tell, Truman Capote's Holly Golightly and Emile Zola's Nana notwithstanding). Sometimes they prefer to describe themselves as "escorts". "Courtesan" was a description I had suggested to my latest client as part of the proposed book title. I thought it sounded rather romantic and redolent with historical connotations. She liked the sound of it until she looked it up in the dictionary and decided that she would rather be described as a "mistress".

Books can also provide interesting insights into the thinking that has led these authors to follow their chosen paths through life.

"I told you she was an interesting woman," I said.

"I really couldn't say," my wife said, chucking the vegetables into a pan of boiling water with a dangerous splash. "She just said that and then hung up."

Deathbed delivery

Until the relatively recent proliferation of self-publishing and print-on-demand services, getting a book published was a mind-numbingly slow process. If I started working with someone in January it might well be June before we had managed to get a publisher on board, even with the help of an agent. The publisher would probably then schedule publication the following summer, or maybe even the autumn. It would then take a while for the book to seep into the shops and into the consciousness of the sort of readers who might be likely to recommend it to other people. Eighteen months, therefore, could easily elapse between the first meeting between me (the ghost) and the author and the book actually starting to rise above the horizon.

As a result it is always rather unnerving when the would-be author is of a great age. People of a great age often have the best stories, but they are nearly always in a hurry, fearful that their health will give out before they have had a chance to see their stories in print and enjoy the excitement of being published authors.

Helen-Alice Dear was only 15 when she left London to visit Bulgaria on a family holiday in 1937. Just weeks after her arrival, she found herself unable to leave and struggling to survive in an increasingly hostile and terrifying environment, first under the Nazis and then the Russians. Her marriage to a Bulgarian man bore her four children but they were often homeless, cold and hungry. Despite these hardships, Helen refused to give up hope and bravely managed to protect and raise four happy children. When the Berlin Wall fell in 1989, she was finally able to fulfil her dream of returning to her homeland. She was a woman of indomitable spirit but as she approached 85 even her strength was beginning to fade.

With the help of one of her daughters I wrote a synopsis and found an agent and a publisher. Things were moving forward smoothly by publishing standards, but agonisingly slowly for Helen as her health continued to slip away.

The book — *My Family is All I Have* — was printed but still sitting in the publisher's warehouse when Helen's daughter rang to tell me that her mother was in hospital and the outlook was not good. There were hurried phone calls and a dash to the publisher's office where I was able to snatch the first copies of the book from the editor's desk before grabbing a cab to the hospital in time to line them up on the table stretching over Helen's bed. Her own youthful face stared down at her from the front covers.

"Do you think it looks all right?" she asked, her smile suggesting she had already decided that it did.

The following day she passed away.

The mid-book blues

Writing books is one of the most enjoyable and rewarding ways to earn a living and I can't imagine ever doing anything else. That does not mean, however, that every part of the operation is a joy. As with any large-scale endeavour, from creating a garden to running a marathon, from being a rock star to being a prince of the realm, there are times where the effort and the monotony of the job feel crushing.

The blues usually strike me about half way through the writing process. All too often, I believe, the books which the market has traditionally demanded are longer than their subject matter merits. If you write tightly and edit well as you go along you can often tell a story very effectively in 30,000 to 50,000 words (*The Turn of the Screw, Animal Farm, Of Mice and Men, The Great Gatsby, Death in Venice, Heart of Darkness, The Picture of Dorian Gray* . . . I could go on). Publishers and readers, however, have been accustomed for many years to books that are 80,000 to 150,000 words — and sometimes longer. Designed originally to work well as parcels in the American postal system at the end of the nineteenth century, they are simply the size and shape that people have grown used to and, therefore, expect.

Imagine that you have been commissioned to write a blockbuster thriller which will go out under the name of a famous author who always produces books that are at least 400 pages long (around 150,000 words). The plot that has been worked out is great, the characters are strong and you've managed to tell the whole thing very succinctly and elegantly in 50,000 words.

That is the morning when you wake up to the realisation that you now have to find another hundred thousand words without ruining the tension, without losing the attention of the readers and without waffling.

Waffling is easy, of course, and by no means an unpleasant way to earn a living, but if you do that you will only have to go back and cut it all out again later, losing thousands of valuable words and dozens of valuable man-hours and severely endangering your will to live.

Like any marathon runner you have to put your head down and keep powering on, but you then become obsessed with word-counts: constantly checking how many words you have done that day (or in the last ten minutes), working out how many more days you need if you continue at that rate, forcing yourself to stay at the screen for just one more hour, then just one more, agonising every time you have to cut something out and the word-count drops by even a few dozen. The days seem to stretch out ahead for ever.

Like the marathon runner, however, and the patient gardener, perseverance and professionalism always pay off and you eventually come out of the darkness of winter into the sunshine once more. The finishing line comes in sight and you are able to sprint to the end, refreshed by the rush of adrenaline and the bloom of another spring, ready and enthusiastic to start on the next book, all memories of the blue days forgotten.

Maybe this is a good moment to confess to another sin: the sin of envy. I can't help but imagine how glorious it must be to be one of those immortal songwriters who you hear talking about how they penned their most famous track in a matter of minutes, creating a perfect little masterpiece that will be paying them and their descendants royalties for years to come. Imagine for a moment being Ray Davies and dashing off masterpieces like "Waterloo Sunset", "Lola" and "Sunny Afternoon". Not only do you then have the rest of the day to please yourself, you also get to sing your stories in front of hundreds of thousands of adoring fans. Contrast that with the long haul of the book writer who is then lucky if he can persuade half a dozen people to turn up to a reading in a bookshop. Envious? I'm positively mint green.

Addiction to charts

More than once I have allowed myself to become as addicted to watching the bestseller charts as I am to gin, caffeine and emails; desperate all the time for a new fix, even though I know it will inevitably lead to another painful comedown.

I can completely understand why ego-crazed pop stars are driven tantrum mad when some giant-selling track from a rival act squats at the top of the charts for months on end, forever depriving them of the ultimate glory they believe to be their right. To be number two or three is great, of course, but to be able to label your book merely "a *Sunday Times* bestseller" is never going to be the same as being "a number one bestseller".

So many times I have ghosted a potential chart topper, only to be held off the top spot by some other mega-selling celebrity author or freak hit from household names like Jeremy Clarkson and Jamie Oliver, Bill Bryson and Sharon Osbourne, Katie Price and Alex Ferguson, Barack Obama and One Direction (not to mention the Bible, the Highway Code and *Who Moved My Cheese?*).

I know my addiction is illogical, that a book which sells a thousand copies a week for 20 years and never features in any charts is an infinitely better earner than one that surges out of the starting gate with a 10,000 sale in the first week and has completely petered out by the end of the year. I know it because I have had those too, but I am still addicted to the adrenaline rush of the quick number one surge. The pleasures and rewards of sensible moderation are subtler and require a degree of patience that I always have difficulty in mastering whenever the painful yearning for personal validation takes hold.

More dangerous even than the charts in newspapers like the *Sunday Times*, the *New York Times*, *Publishers Weekly* and *The Bookseller*, are the Amazon rankings. This is a virtual casino that feeds both my paranoia and my normally suppressed ego as a writer in a dizzying, aerobatic display of highs and lows. Where the printed charts only provide weekly fixes I can now get fresh highs and lows every few hours by logging onto Amazon and looking up any one of the titles that I have a vested interest in.

As with all drugs, you take your first hit out of curiosity, thinking that you can handle it. You see that your "sales rank" is pleasantly high — let's say you are at number 1,000. Thinking this is a good omen you go back the next day to see if you have climbed any higher — you have, you are now down to three figures. You experience a ludicrously pleasant rush of optimism and now they've got you.

The next time you tune in you have plummeted, maybe in the space of just a few hours, to number 10,000. How can this be? You are immediately filled with angst. Has your publisher failed to send them a new order? Has a bad review appeared somewhere and halted sales in their tracks? Or are you simply doomed to a future of abject failure, your children destined to beg on the streets?

You tentatively go back in a few hours later and, miracle of miracles, you are back in three figures. You are high again, thrilled with yourself and the world. Now you are Amazon's slave. It will only be a matter of time before you are unable to stop yourself from checking in almost every hour. It will become a new distraction from the job of writing as irresistible as making another cup of coffee (each cup a little stronger than the last, but that's another story).

Tales from below stairs

When someone introduces themselves over the phone with one of the most famous names on the planet, it can be disorienting. The call had come late in the evening from Hollywood, at a time of day when it was a surprise for the phone to ring at all. My brain, comfortably addled by supper, gin and television, had difficulty clicking onto an entirely new track at a moment's notice. The name sounded eerily familiar but I couldn't think why. Then I remembered that it was the name of an extremely famous film star, but assumed that this must be someone else with the same name. *Then* I remembered the connection and tried to work out what she was talking about.

That whole mental process was probably no more than a few seconds and was probably indiscernible to the woman on the other end of the line, who appeared to be angry before the conversation even began.

"We've received this manuscript from the Johnsons," she said and the whole thing clicked into place.

Mr and Mrs Johnson had worked for this star and her even-more-famous film star husband. Mrs Johnson had been their housekeeper when they were at their house in England while Mr Johnson had been the chauffeur and general handyman. They had approached me because they wanted to tell an affectionate insiders' tale of life with one of the most celebrated Hollywood couples. It had been a pleasant if uncontroversial story and I thought the fame of their employers might be enough to get the Johnsons a publishing deal. I interviewed them and produced a synopsis. Throughout history servants have been a rich source of material for writers of both fiction and non-fiction. They often get to places the rest of us can never hope to see, and sometimes have front row seats at historic events.

"Before we send this to any agents or publishers," I told the Johnsons, "you need to get it cleared by your former employers."

"That'll be fine," they said. "We get on really well. They're more like friends than employers."

"Should be fine then," I agreed, and promptly forgot about the whole thing as I was in the middle of writing something else. I assumed there would be a short hiatus and then the stars would give their blessing to this friendly little project. I certainly hadn't expected that Mrs Megastar would feel sufficiently incensed to put in a call herself — usually incensed megastars get their lawyers to write letters.

"I don't know what they're thinking," she said. "There's no way we want the details of our home life published in a book. If we wanted to do that we'd write it ourselves. They signed confidentiality contracts when we took them on so they can't do it anyway . . ."

Fortunately the would-be authors had told her that it was my idea that they should ask permission before continuing with the project, and she was grateful to me for that, but listening to her perfectly justified indignation I realised that she and her husband had a very different idea of their relationship with the Johnsons. Just because they had been "friendly" towards them while they were in their employ, they had never at any stage thought of themselves as "friends" with the couple. The social chasm between "upstairs" and "downstairs" had not really moved that far from where it had been a century before. Once she had vented her fury and realised that I was agreeing with everything she said, she calmed down, promised to contact me if she ever decided to tell her own story and the entire project melted away.

Employees of the rich and famous often go looking for ghostwriters and sometimes they do have stories of genuine interest. Princess Diana's publicity-hungry butler was perhaps the most vivid example of the breed and there have been many other royal tales from nannies, housekeepers, bodyguards, interior decorators and illegitimate children who want their illustrious lineage to be acknowledged.

It's astonishing how many of history's alpha males sired children with the women who worked for them. Arnold Schwarzenegger merely joined onto the end of a long conga line when he admitted to having a son with his family's housekeeper. The Lord alone knows how far the European royal families have spread their DNA through the families of those who have worked for them.

If people work in service industries like the hotel business or limousine hire or security they can often write generic exposés of their employers and there is also a market for stories about life "below stairs" in private houses (the "Downton Abbey Syndrome" perhaps), and I guess you could say this book falls into this category.

The best of these stories can be delicious concoctions of gossip and social observation and can provide an insight into how life works in households that are very different to those of most of their readers . . . but most aren't.

A confession of cowardice

Writing a book in someone else's voice allows the ghostwriter to abdicate responsibility for anything that is said. The release from that responsibility compensates for the inability to express your own views. In one way it makes it easier to tell a story dramatically and to introduce readers to the personality of the subject, but it is also an act of cowardice, a way of hiding behind a mask. It makes it much easier to express outrageous opinions, to justify shocking behaviour, if you are using someone else's voice and letting them face any hostile responses that might come from readers.

Maybe it is the same with fiction. Some stories would be hard to tell effectively without a narrator. Would Vladimir Nabokov have been able to make *Lolita* palatable if he had viewed Humbert, Lolita's seducer, objectively? By allowing Humbert to be the teller of the story he could make it easier for the reader to understand why the man acted as he did, perhaps even to empathise with him despite the fact that his crime would be despicable to virtually everyone. The glamour and drama of life at Brideshead and Jay Gatsby's mansion were all the more evocative for having been viewed through the eyes of the impressionable young narrators, Charles Ryder and Nick Carraway, who were actually there and actually affected by the events that occurred.

By taking on the role of a ghost, the writer is effectively, and perhaps cravenly, handing over responsibility for the truth to the narrator or client.

Writing in two voices at once

Sometimes a story can be most effectively told by taking more than one viewpoint. I've written several books where we have alternated between two or more voices. There was a couple who wanted to write about the man's ordeal as an inmate in a third world prison and his girlfriend's struggle to get him released. We were able to move the reader between the shocking details of the man's experiences inside a cramped, airless prison cell shared with a dozen others, and the desperate story of his girlfriend who could find no way to reach out to her partner. By cutting back and forth you can achieve much the same effect as a film director might employ to tell such a story.

In another book I wrote for two girls who were travelling together when their plane was hi-jacked and crash landed in the sea. They both had roughly the same story to tell of their near-death experiences, but by alternating their voices we were able to see events through the eyes of two different personalities. If told from just one perspective there probably would not have been enough words for a full-length book.

In another bestselling book, *My Secret Sister*, ghosted by Jacquie Buttriss, siblings separated at birth and put up for adoption told parallel stories of their lives and their long searches for one another in two distinct voices, until they eventually came together at the end of the story — a narrative trick worthy of a bestselling novelist.

Just a single copy

He had spent his life travelling the world and trading, building a mighty conglomerate of companies, most of them market leaders in their sectors but none of them household names and none of their products remotely sexy. He was 60 years old and his only daughter had just presented him with his first grandson, who had been named after him.

He couldn't help himself from beaming with pride as he passed a photograph of the boy across the lunch table at his club in Pall Mall.

"When he is 40," he said, "and I am long gone, and he visits his mother and asks what exactly Grandpa did to make so much money, I want her to be able to send him to her library where this book will be waiting for him. We only need to print up one copy, but it must be done beautifully and it will tell him all the things I would be able to tell him if he was sitting here with me now. I want to tell him about my parents and my grandparents, about where they came from and what they did to help me get started, and then I want to explain how I built the company."

He was under no illusion that the book would ever be of interest to the general public, although I did convince him that it would be worth printing up a few dozen copies so that it could go into various archives within the company as well, for the use of future historians. In essence, however, all he wanted was an 80,000 word letter to his grandson. It was a joy to be working with such a specific and achievable brief, not having to worry about finding agents or publishers or scheming how to get it into the shops and the charts.

Family secrets

"Hah!" My wife's jubilant exclamation jerked me back from the reverie I had drifted into with the aid of the fire crackling in the grate, the television burbling in the background and the gin numbing the anxieties of the day. "I knew it!"

"What did you know?"

"You have criminal genes. I just knew it. Convicts!"

One of my wife's addictions, every bit as debilitating as my own mild fondnesses, is to stalking ancestors who previously believed they were resting in peace. During many happy hours on the laptop (and a considerable number of visits to libraries and other archives), she managed to dig up her own relatives back to the dawn of time and then set about mine. Through my father's line she discovered the extraordinarily colourful family of a Victorian Archbishop of Canterbury and some alarmingly close intermarriages within a limited number of families including that of Charles Darwin. I believe limited gene pools, particularly in his own family, was one of the great man's prime worries, and a tendency to despondency at best and complete madness at worst seemed to dog many of the stories

238

she was uncovering with such glee. She had now started on my mother's lineage, finding a family that had made a healthy fortune by setting up a trading company in Australia, a fortune which was frittered away and had disappeared without trace two generations later.

"Your great, great grandparents," she was peering closely at her laptop screen, trying to make out handwriting two centuries old, "or maybe there should be another 'great' in there … anyway, they ran an illegal still in Scotland. An inspector from Customs and Excise confiscated it and they attacked him with an iron bar as he was loading it onto his cart to take away. They were both arrested, tried and sent to Australia on separate convict ships. She gave birth on the trip down. When they got there they were reunited and put to work for a man who owned a massive sheep farm. Your great, great, whatever grandfather then died and his widow married the sheep farmer, her children inheriting the whole thing." She sat back triumphantly. "I knew it!"

I relate this tale of unseemly gloating because my wife is not alone in her addiction. The internet has made it possible for thousands of people, alerted by television programmes such as *Who Do You Think You Are?*, to dig out stories about their families. Many of them need the help of ghostwriters to put these stories into a form where they can become family heirlooms, keeping voices that would previously have disappeared into the grave with their owners alive down the centuries.

When I was a teenager my mother wrote a short memoir of growing up in the thirties. Being an arrogant adolescent with my eyes fixed on my own glorious literary future I paid her labours scant attention and she was far too modest to do more than simply type them up and leave them in a drawer. After her death, however, when I started to wonder about how her life might have been before my father and I came into it, the book — now printed and published privately by a cousin who recognised its value before I did — has been an enormous source of answers. I only wish my father, grandparents and all who came before them had done the same. Such books might only ever be of interest to a few dozen people, but their relevance to that small audience is likely to be as strong as, or even stronger than, any famous and feted work of literature.

One for the bank vaults

The lady asked me to meet her at an Italian restaurant just behind Knightsbridge but she wouldn't give me her name. She told me she would book the table in my name. The restaurant was discreet and intimate, the tablecloths thick, smooth and gleaming white, the cutlery heavy and the wine glasses as light as feathers. The staff members were equally discreet. I presume that they were used to catering for trysts and liaisons.

Her accent on the phone had been precise and upper class. She might not be English by birth but she had almost certainly been to an English boarding school. When she arrived I was surprised that she appeared younger than I had pictured. It was hard to imagine what her background might be. Her ancestors might have come from India or South America, or both. Most likely she was the result of several generations of high-level global mixing. Whatever her history the result took my breath away. I was pretty sure that I recognised her face from the society pages of glossy magazines, but I still had no idea who she might be.

Her manners were immaculate but she was wary, like a wild animal, apparently unsure whether I was going to turn out to be friend or foe. The waiters came and went from the table and she slowly relaxed. As she allowed snippets of her story to emerge bells rang in various compartments of my memory. I recalled seeing her pictured with a much older husband in the society pages of glossy magazines. I remembered that there was some sort of divorce being threatened and a great deal of money was at stake, as well as the custody of children. There was an estate and an inheritance, which included a stately home and some dispute over the paternity of the children in the marriage.

"I think it will be hard to sell this to a publisher while the divorce and the court case are still under way," I warned. "The legal difficulties would make them very nervous."

"It is of no importance," she said. "I just want to have my story written down and then we can put it in a bank vault. I want it to be there for my children to read later so that they will know my side of the story, and I want my husband and his lawyers to know that the book exists."

"Blackmail?" I asked, laughing in an attempt to take the sting out of the word.

"Insurance," she corrected me, flashing a row of perfect white teeth.

It seemed that we had connected successfully.

"We have a house in Villefranche," she said. "There's only the housekeeper down there at this time of year so we won't be disturbed. How long would we need to spend together?"

"A week would be fine."

"And you don't mind that I may be the only person ever to read the manuscript?"

"It's you I'm writing it for. As long as you are happy with it then I will be happy with it."

Several months later, once the book had been written and safely deposited in the bank, and the lawyers had finished wrangling, I read that she had received one of the largest divorce settlements ever.

On behalf of my client

"She said what?" My wife's tone of voice managed to convey both her contempt for the woman I was describing and her astonishment at my naivety for swallowing her line. Her fork had come to a halt half way to her mouth as she peered down the table at me, obviously awaiting some sort of satisfactory response.

As so often happens I had been talking without fully engaging my brain, expounding my client's theories on why she was performing a social service by sleeping with other people's husbands. My wife's tone had woken me fully and I sensed danger. I paused and struggled to replay whatever I had just said in my head. The words, which just an hour or two before I had been typing out with fluent conviction, suddenly had a rather hollow ring to them.

I cleared my throat and tried putting my client's point of view a little differently. My wife listened like a High Court judge might listen to a lawyer pleading for a client with a hopeless case, but her expression did not lighten.

"And you believed her?" she asked once I had burbled to a standstill.

Now I was on the ropes. I had to think why it was I was putting forward this woman's highly immoral ideas as if they were founded in logic. Under this sort of cross-examination my client's view of the world did seem a little ethically shaky, but as her ghost it was my job to put her case for her as eloquently and convincingly as possible, not challenge it. If I had actually questioned what she was telling me to her face she would have grown defensive and would have become more cautious in talking to me honestly. I needed her to open up and explain herself as fully as possible; I did not want to intimidate her into silence or aggressive self-justification.

Under my wife's inquisitorial glare, however, I could feel my confidence in my client's story ebbing away. I was still only in the early stages of the writing and I couldn't afford to lose sympathy with the woman whose voice I was going to be thinking and speaking in for the next few months.

"I can't talk about it," I said, able to hear the panic in my own voice.

"What do you mean?"

"I have to believe in her version of the story if I am going to be able to tell it convincingly. Once I've finished the book we can argue about the rights and wrongs of her philosophy of life as much as we like. I just can't do it now."

My wife gave a snort which could have been simply agreement but to my sensitive ears still seemed to contain a suggestion of derision. A new golden rule had just been born in our house.

A movie star and her entourage

A-listers in every walk of life, from movie stars to political leaders, billionaires to sports stars, are nearly always easy to get on with. It is the people who stand between them and the rest of the world who sometimes make life arduous.

The ferocious doctor's receptionist has become a cliché, but there is a reason why such people are hired and vested with power; it is so that their bosses never have to fall out with anyone, never have to seem impatient or obstructive because their Rottweilers do all that for them. The bigger the star, the more ferocious the Rottweilers that stand between them and the rest of us.

If you have been hired by a big star to be their manager/agent/lawyer/publicist, then you have to make sure that you are seen to be doing something for your salary. In some cases that "something" can be arranging unnecessary meetings, writing unnecessarily long letters, drawing up unnecessarily complex contracts and generally making everything take twice as long as it should.

In an ideal world a great film star would decide that she wanted to write a book and needed a ghost. She

246

would ask someone to provide her with a few names and then either she would ring herself for a chat or she would ask her people to set up a meeting. If things went well then the lawyers could be asked to draw up a contract.

What actually happened in one case is symptomatic of the whole business. Someone junior from the star's management team rang to enquire as to whether, in principle, I would be free to write a book for someone "very important" who couldn't be named. When I answered in the affirmative a long confidentiality agreement was drawn up before I could be told who she was. A meeting was then arranged, but not with her. Before that I had to be vetted to ensure that it was safe to allow me into her presence. On the day the people who were supposed to be at the meeting were held up at another more important one, and when they did arrive they were unable to give the matter enough time to make a decision. Another meeting was arranged and the same thing happened. Eventually they decided I could be introduced to the star.

Another meeting was arranged at the hotel she was staying at while passing through Paris on a press junket to promote a film. Getting there on time I found I had to meet first with someone from the management company, her personal assistant, a lawyer and a publicist, and a parallel team from the film company.

Eventually I was shown into a room that the star would soon be passing through on her way from one appointment to another. I was not the only one waiting in the room. There was also a journalist who had been promised an interview, a hairdresser, a make-up artist and a team from one of the couture houses who had some frocks for her to try on in preparation for a premiere later that night. She would not be actually watching the film, merely walking up the red carpet for the benefit of the assembled media cameras and then walking straight through the cinema to be let out of a back door, where a car would be waiting to whisk her away, which was just as well since some of the dresses did not look like their elaborate folds would respond well to being crammed into a cinema seat for a couple of hours.

When the lady herself eventually swept in several hours later, surrounded by a number of other people with earpieces and clipboards, the grooming squad fell into place around her, working on her hair and her face and showing her dresses as she listened to the people with clipboards, one of whom brought me forward for an introduction.

If she had ever known that she was going to be writing a book, she had forgotten, but that did not dent her charm or her politeness. She chatted for as long as she could before she had to try on a dress and it was suggested that I should wait in another room in order to continue the conversation later. By the time they remembered that I was in the other room our star had swept off to the premiere.

From that short exchange, however, she had decided that it would be fine to go ahead with the project, but that required me to be passed back into the hands of the managers and lawyers so that everything could be finalised. Over the following months I spent more hours in meetings and on phone calls with assistants than I would have needed to write the entire book if I had just been engaged for the job on day one. The star herself, however, was a joy from start to finish but the book, being micro-managed as it was by everyone who had a public relations stake in the lady's career and image, was never going to catch the imagination of the book-reading public. It sold to fans in the same way that a poster of the star might sell and no doubt it did exactly the brand reinforcement job that they required.

A hit-man comes to lunch

I prefer to travel to the authors rather than have them coming to me, mainly because it puts them more at ease if they are on their own home territory. It is also easier for me to concentrate on the job of questioning and listening if I am not thinking all the time about whether I am being a good enough host. On this occasion, however, the author in question was between abodes and didn't have anywhere suitable for us to meet.

My wife, who had some sort of domestic crisis under way, had not had time to ask any questions about who it might be with me in the front room that morning and was out when he arrived, returning in time to pop her head round the door and enquire if we would like a little lunch.

By the time we got to the kitchen she had laid everything up very prettily, being something of a domestic goddess in these matters, never able to do anything less than perfectly, and I introduced her to the amiable old man who followed me into the room.

I could see she was only half listening as we continued to chat, her mind on other matters until certain phrases seeped through whatever else she was thinking about and brought her eyes into focus. Gangster family names such as "Kray" and "Richardson" were being mentioned, as they so often are by Londoners of a certain age, and then our lunch guest made the casual comment, "so I had to clip him", and her puzzlement seemed to clear.

I swear I could see a light coming on in her eyes before she quickly looked down at her plate and collected her thoughts, piecing together other things I had told her over the previous few weeks about a client who had been involved with the criminal gangs of south and east London; violent men who ruled Soho and much of the West End during the fifties and sixties. There had been a spate of these gangster stories being published after the success of a book called *The Guv'nor* by Lenny McLean, which came out at the end of the nineties. None of them came anywhere near to matching the sales of *The Guv'nor*, including the tale that we were working on that day. It found a publisher but it did not catch the reading public's attention.

Fortunately our guest was happily launched on a string of stories and my wife had time to compose herself before she needed to ask if he was ready for some pudding.

Writers as parasites

There is something of the parasite about all writers, but ghostwriters particularly. I have always been more comfortable being a spectator at life's feast rather than a participant, allowing other people to have the adventures and face the dangers and horrors that I then write about from the safety of my own home.

It was always thus. At school I did everything I could to avoid team sports, as horrified by the socialising that surrounded them as I was by the pointlessness of the sports themselves. How can you think freely, daydream and ask questions in the middle of a game of rugby when you are in imminent danger of being brought painfully to the ground? Once, while batting in a school cricket game, I was actually hit on the head by the oncoming ball because my mind had wandered in the few seconds it had taken the bowler to run up to the wicket and launch his missile in my direction.

Upon arriving in London at 17 I wanted to see and hear everything that was going on in the adult world which seemed to be changing so fast, poke my nose into as many corners of life as possible, while at the same time always being nervous about actually participating. Luckily I had a school friend who shared my curiosity but not my reticence. Born with no apparent ability to assess risks of any sort, he was willing to try everything and happy for me to tag along and observe. With all the merry amorality of a male teenager he would steal brazenly from the shops where he found employment, went begging on the London railway stations when short of cash and cheerfully sold his services in fetid little amusement arcades around Piccadilly Circus, despite having developed rabidly heterosexual preferences. I fear I may have egged this real-life Artful Dodger on in all his interesting endeavours simply to collect more information and experiences that I would later be able to draw upon for writing.

In the end he took one risk too many and died dramatically before even out of his teens, falling from the window of my fourth floor flat while apparently under the drug-induced impression that he could fly, while I lived on. It was my first brush with the sobering finality of death.

But isn't "living on" one of the features of a parasite? My dictionary defines the word as: "any organism that grows, feeds and is sheltered on or in a different organism while contributing nothing to the survival of its host." That seems about right.

Ordinary people who do extraordinary things

One of the privileges of ghostwriting is getting to meet people who achieve extraordinary things in circumstances that I believe would leave me utterly defeated. You only have to think of some of the athletes who compete in the Paralympics to get what I mean, but it isn't always a physical obstacle that sets the challenge and forces people to achieve superhuman feats of courage and determination, it can just as easily be an emotional one.

It never ceases to amaze me, for instance, how anyone copes with the loss of a child, particularly if that loss happens under exceptionally traumatic conditions. In 2006 I was introduced to Ann Ming, a former nurse who discovered the decomposing body of her murdered daughter, Julie, three months after the police had given up searching for her.

A violent local man was then arrested and tried for Julie's murder but a series of blunders allowed him to walk free. Knowing he could not be tried again under the law of "double jeopardy", he callously bragged about his "perfect crime". But he had reckoned without

Ann who set about campaigning to overturn the 800-year-old rule, which had been enshrined in the Magna Carta. She managed to confront the highest in the land and eventually succeeded in having the law changed, ensuring that her daughter's murderer could be retried and punished for his crime.

It has been an honour to meet several people like Ann and to help them tell their stories. People who have resolutely refused to allow the great cruelties of life to defeat them.

Leaving London

I never really wanted to leave London once I got there, but I guess everyone has to grow up and buy a house and a washing machine sometime. I'd been living in the city for more than a dozen years and had ended up renting a flat beside the river in Chiswick, the waters at high tide lapping just yards from the window where I stationed myself and my typewriter every day.

The flat was in the home of an elderly widow whose husband had been curator of antiques at the Victoria and Albert Museum and one of whose sons was a Cabinet Minister in Margaret Thatcher's government. Our flat had once been the family's "nursery wing" and the surrounding house was a wonderland of cobwebs and curiosities. I would quite happily have sat there, watching the waters flow by, for the rest of my life.

Our landlady, however, turned out to be mortal and passed away after we had been there five years. The family needed to sell the elegant old house to someone who would then brush away the cobwebs and make it worth millions, and there was little chance that we would ever find somewhere comparable in London for the money we had been paying. (I suspect the family had deliberately and discreetly allowed our rent to remain low in exchange for the peace of mind of knowing that there were sympathetic young people around the house as their mother grew increasingly frail.) The thought of moving back into the world of damp basements in rundown areas was now less appealing than it had been during the earlier stages of my adult adventure.

It was time to get serious, move to the country, become a property owner, start a family and worry about things like the roof blowing off on windy nights or passing herds of deer stripping the shrubberies.

There are huge compensations to bringing up a family in the country but I have to admit I still feel a sort of peace descending on me when the train back to London crosses over the waters that I used to watch flowing past my window, and releases me into the familiar streets of my youth. New York, Hong Kong, Paris, Sydney: they all have their different charms and excitements but it is London, the city that I first read about and dreamed about and visited on steam trains with my mother, that eventually draws me back.

Despite all the developments to the east of the city, the West End and its surrounding areas stay remarkably unchanged. The influx of the global wealthy, initially from the oil-rich states of the Middle East, followed by oligarchs from Russia and the rest of the world, has cleaned up streets that were once mean, turned mews houses into property goldmines and breathed life into mansions that had become shabby office spaces. The great spending booms have revived some shops, while the internet has crushed others, and the growth of 24-hour café culture has given many of the streets a continental feel, even on chilly English evenings.

My parents set up their first married home in the city at the end of the forties, in the aftermath of the Blitz. By the time I arrived there from school in 1970 there were still bombsites in evidence and Covent Garden was still the Dickensian fruit and veg market that George Bernard Shaw had depicted in *Pygmalion*, and which the film version, *My Fair Lady*, had just started to glamorise and sanitise. The dark, abandoned warehouses that loomed over the river from its southern banks had become the haunt of squatting artists and would not start to be converted into multi-million pound apartments for at least another 10 years.

As a freelance journalist I wrote a newspaper for St Katharine Docks, the first of the docks to be gentrified by property speculators, and chronicled the changes as one of the greatest historical cities in the world adapted and regenerated from its sea-trading, bomb-battered past, moving towards its digital-trading future. From the squalor of Dickens's East End to the grandeur of Byron's Piccadilly, from Bertie Wooster's Mayfair, Peter Pan's Kensington and Paddington Bear's Notting Hill to today's city as depicted by authors as various as Jake Arnott, John Lanchester, Zadie Smith and Ian McEwan, London's magic continues to haunt the pages of books and my children are now able to live comfortably in areas of the city which were virtually derelict in the seventies, while the areas where I lived have become too expensive for most young people to even contemplate.

Soft times

When I'm travelling as a writer to strange and distant lands my conscience tells me that I should be living like the indigenous people. I should be experiencing whatever privations and discomforts they are suffering on a daily basis in order to fully absorb the colour and patina of their lives. If that involves a lack of running water, cooking a sparse dinner over an open fire and encountering insects that make your nights a waking nightmare, then so be it. I've read enough from authors like Wilfred Thesiger, Jan Morris and Paul Theroux to know how a real travel writer should throw themselves into the moment.

Sometimes, of course, that is exactly what happens and it is often a highly rewarding experience — at least it is once you are safely home and looking back through your memories. (Graham Greene, after all, was almost finished off by illness while travelling in search of his own version of Joseph Conrad's *Heart of Darkness* in Liberia in 1935, but lived on to become one of the greatest writers of his generation.)

I have to confess, however, that the more strange and distant the lands I am visiting, the more I relish having a base in an anonymous, international, five star hotel. The hot shower so powerful it massages out the muscles that have become knotted with the bumpy roads of the day at the same time as shooting away the dust; the air-conditioning that lowers the body temperature; the ability to make yourself understood in your own language and the bland international breakfast and strong coffee that set the stomach up for a day of local delicacies. It is the very blandness and anonymity of these hotel chains that soothes the nerves and provides comfort for the body and the mind after a long day of often violent stimulation.

I do, however, feel guilty whenever I find myself scampering back to the five star safety of an international hotel chain, but then I tell myself that even Greene ended his days in Antibes, possibly one of the most comfortable and civilised places in the world, far from the "Heart of Darkness" he once sought out so eagerly.

A pain in Baguio

The pain woke me in the middle of the night, like a knife had been rammed into the lower part of my back. I was in a hotel in Baguio, in the middle of the Philippines. I had been travelling with a government guide, retracing the life story of Ferdinand Marcos, the country's President, as part of the same vague, unspecified public relations brief that had led me to lunching with his wife in Manila. I had no idea whether the guide was staying in the same hotel; she had merely made sure I was checked in before disappearing for the night.

Until the day before I had been with a group of journalists on an "educational", but the others had now flown home and I had gone on with my guide to do more research. In the dark and quiet of the tropical night I suddenly felt very alone as the pain repeated in steady waves.

I pulled myself out of bed and tried moving around the room to see if it was a muscular cramp of some sort. It abated for a few moments and then returned with greater severity, almost knocking me off my feet and making me feel nauseous. It was time to ask for help. I phoned down and enquired if there was a doctor attached to the hotel. A few hours later I had been given an injection and the pain had magically lifted.

When my exquisitely groomed government minder arrived at breakfast time to escort me wherever we were due to go to next I told her of my night's adventures. She listened with a serious level of concentration and when I had finished she raised one immaculate eyebrow.

"Could it possibly have anything to do with the things you got up to in Manila?"

It was a fair cop, if a rather dubious medical diagnosis. On one of our days touring round Manila we had been taken to a beach where a gentleman from the London *Times* (with whom I had been designated to share a room) and I had been approached by a young man selling weed. Despite the disapproving looks we had received from the rest of the group, and from our minders, we had made a purchase and later settled down in our hotel room to enjoy the goods before dinner.

That night was to be an official banquet to mark the end of the tour for the other journalists and some important person was coming from the other end of the country to meet me and brief me on whatever it was I was going to be doing on the next leg of my trip.

Up to that point I hadn't had much more than schoolboy experiences with drugs and I was not prepared for the strength of whatever it was we were happily puffing on as we sat on our balcony overlooking the beach, serenaded by the waves and the cicadas. By the time I realised that I was high as a satellite it was too late to do anything about it apart from giggle and talk nonsense. Aware enough to know that I needed to sober up if I was going to make sensible dinner table conversation, I decided to have a cold shower. That might have helped if alcohol had been the problem but the only effect it had that evening was to make my hair stick out from my head at right angles.

Not bothering to look in a mirror I decided that I was now in a fit state to present myself and floated to the banquet as if everything was normal. It was only as I started to come gently down from the clouds an hour or so later that I realised everyone around me had been having considerable difficulty following whatever it was I had been babbling about. With the immaculate politeness that characterises so many people in the Far East no one had mentioned that they had noticed anything, until the moment I owned up to my night-time pain.

The rest of the trip passed uneventfully and a kidney stone finally worked its way agonisingly through my system once I was safely back in England. It almost seemed like a fitting punishment for my transgressions.

Whoring myself again

I hadn't heard my son coming into the office as I typed away at some self-promotional piece of blogging or tweeting or whatever was the social media flavour of that day. He only needed to stand behind me for a moment to grasp what I was doing, being a world-class reader of screens.

"Whoring yourself again?" he enquired cheerfully before ambling off to the kitchen to stare into the fridge for a while.

The bluntness of his comic timing made me laugh, as it often does, then I got to thinking. "Whoring yourself again" is pretty much the perfect definition of freelance life. I've spent time with a great many people who have at some stage been involved in prostitution, either voluntarily or enforced. You sell your body or you sell your brain — either way you run the risk of ending up selling your soul.

Most writers hate promoting themselves, always hoping that publishers or agents or critics or fans will do it for them. But in our hearts we all know if we wait for other people to sing our praises and rush out to buy our wares we are going to starve to death, so we hitch up our skirts and return to the kerbside of life.

The suppression of the ego

"Have just swum round hotel pool," my youngest daughter texted from Zante, where she was indulging in her first non-family holiday. "Saw four different people reading your books. So annoying that I can't tell them my dad wrote them!"

Virtually everyone, from Mariella Frostrup, the Queen of Radio Book Shows, to the proverbial bloke in the pub, wants to know the same thing about the battered egos of ghostwriters. "Isn't it frustrating to have a book at the top of the bestseller lists and for no one to know that you wrote it?"

"I think it's a matter of expectations," is my usual reply. "If I had written a book expecting it to be published in my own name and to bring me great glory, then I would be very disappointed — perhaps even bitter — if the publisher informed me at the last moment that it was going to go out under the name of a footballer or soap actor. But if I know that is what I have been hired to do from the start I am merely pleased to see that I have succeeded in achieving the brief I was given. If I had been Barack Obama's speechwriter and a speech that I had written gained him a standing ovation and led to him being praised for his eloquence and getting into the White House I would not feel frustrated that he received the glory rather than me, I would simply be pleased that my speech had done the trick. It's the same with books."

There are, I believe, more positives to being invisible than negatives. While there are always moments when everyone fantasises about being feted and adored, nominated for prizes and fawned over on chat shows, there is also a great deal of comfort in not being someone who had hoped for such things, only to be disappointed. Once I finish a book I can move straight on to another one, immediately immersing myself in a completely new subject and not having to trail around obscure radio stations in the middle of the night to talk about something I wrote a year earlier, or obliged to turn up for bookshop signings only to find that no one is remotely interested. Earning a living as a writer opens you up to enough potential situations for rejection as it is without going out looking for more.

On the subject of Mariella Frostrup, sort of, I was being interviewed at home one day by an outside broadcast team for one of her various bookish television programmes. Asked why I so liked writing in the voices of people of different genders, nationalities and backgrounds to myself, I gave a pat answer which seemed to me like a clever sound bite.

"I am white, male, middle aged, middle class, middle brow and English-speaking," I pontificated to camera. "I think the world has heard enough from people like me over the last few hundred years, don't you? Perhaps it's time to listen to a few other voices."

I thought no more of it until the show was aired. I neither saw nor heard any danger signals as I admired the screen version of myself delivering my smart answer. The item ended and the programme returned to the studio, where Mariella was sitting with Peter James, a kind friend and enormously successful author, and Robert Harris, the man who had so generously quoted me in his ghostwriting thriller.

"So, gentlemen," the mischievous Mariella began, "Andrew Crofts thinks we've heard enough from white, male, middle-aged, middle-class, middle-brow English-speaking authors . . . what do you say to that?"

I thought both the white, male, middle-aged, middle-class, middle-brow, English-speaking writers were extremely forgiving under the circumstances.

The Pope's secret mistress

"Who would you most like to work with if you could choose?" people ask.

I'm not sure I can answer that because the best stories are always the ones you know nothing about until they arrive in your inbox. If someone is already known to you well enough for you to want to work with them on their life story, the chances are you already know a lot about them. Unless they are going to reveal some completely new and secret side to their story it would not be particularly interesting to spend several months of your life on it.

It would have been fun to have been given the access that Andrew Morton had to Princess Diana when she decided to talk for the first time about the realities of being part of the royal family, but revelations that dramatic from people who are already heavily scrutinised by the media are very rare indeed.

The most interesting stories are the ones that come as complete surprises.

"Hi, I am the Pope's secret mistress," would be an opening line that would definitely catch my attention.

A writer's pit

I suspect I am not alone in needing to have a small room or cave all to myself, somewhere where dust can accumulate like tumbleweed and papers can stack up around me with no concession to either logic or the "paperless office". Some writers have sheds, some convert spare bedrooms. My cave was originally a game larder and has the vital ingredient of having windows knocked through three of its walls. Without compulsory daylight there would always be the temptation to opt for hibernation during the bleakest months of winter.

I dare say this primal need for privacy and dominion over a small space started in the womb, was fed by an only-childhood with parents who pretty much left me to my own devices in my bedroom as long as I didn't do anything to actually damage the fabric of the house, and came to fruition at my public school where our small studies were actually known as "pits".

I recently visited one of the few remaining monasteries in England, the spires of which I could once see from the windows of the game larder (the garden has since grown up to screen them), and was shocked by how much I was reminded of school by the monks' cold and spartan cells.

It was in that school pit, which can't have been more than six foot by six foot, that I hid myself away behind a locked door with an upright typewriter in order to bash out my first novel when I should have been studying for A levels. Although that book was never published (no surprises there), I was unknowingly taking the first step on a career path that has lasted ever since.

Recently my adult pit became so cluttered and grubby that my wife launched a pre-emptive strike. I had flown down to the Uganda/Rwanda border for a long weekend of interviewing so she knew I was safely out of the house. She went in like a one-woman television makeover team, replacing stained and ragged carpeting with polished wooden flooring, crumbling cardboard boxes with elegant rows of files. The children stood and watched her labours as she assembled new office furniture late into the night and issued dire warnings about how displeased I would be when I returned to find my sanctuary invaded in this way.

Returning to find my private world transformed was indeed disorienting (especially after a long overnight journey back from the heart of Africa), but at the same time liberating. I felt like I had finally been promoted into an adult world. I gloried in the newly created order and cleanliness despite an illogical nervousness that I would not be able to find vital pieces of paper at moments of importance (I would never have been able to find them anyway in the previous chaos).

Gradually, however, to my shame, I have to confess that the clutter and the dust have returned to cover the clean and polished surfaces, reverting it to a state no different to how it was when I was 16 and avoiding the real world in my pit at school.

Who moved my nuts?

"Have you nicked my glasses cleaning cloth?" I demanded.

"What glasses cleaning cloth?" my wife replied without bothering to look up from her Sudoku puzzle.

"The one I keep on my desk. The really nice big one."

"I don't know what you're talking about."

I decided to leave it. I would catch her out later, polishing her glasses when she thought I wasn't looking. I missed having the cloth within immediate reach whenever I was working and suddenly noticed finger-marks on my glasses. It had also been particularly good for polishing computer and iPad screens.

There are certain things that need to be in the right place so that you don't have to go looking for them and break your concentration while in full creative flow. The most important of these things is a steady supply of nuts and raisins for those moments when sudden pangs of hunger strike and there is no immediate prospect of a meal. That was why I was even more peeved a few days later to find that someone had moved some of my nuts from the open jar and secreted them in a small drawer where I keep paper and calling cards.

"Have you been moving my nuts?" I asked, less sure that this accusation sounded credible.

This time she thought it worth looking up. "Are you mad?" she enquired in a voice that suggested she had already decided what the answer was. "You've probably got mice."

"If I had mice I would have seen signs of droppings," I replied, indignant at the very thought. "Why would I get mice?"

"Because you leave your nuts lying all over the place."

I refused to continue with the conversation and my certainty that I was being targeted in some subtle hate campaign was reinforced a few days later when someone severed the lead on my headphones and dropped the earpieces into the open jar of nuts. This, it seemed to me, was now turning into one of those movies where Michael Douglas ends up being attacked with a knife. Even my wife could see that this latest development was intriguing.

"You must have mice," she said categorically. "I told you, you need to clean up in there."

"There are no droppings," I insisted, certain that man-the-hunter would know if he was being invaded by wild life. "And anyway the cat would have got them."

"The cat is too deaf to hear a dog in clogs coming these days," she pointed out. "You can't rely on her."

The following morning I came into the office to find the cat deeply asleep on my chair and an alarmingly well-nourished mouse staring at me from on top of my keyboard. Although he seemed in no hurry to leave I still failed to get him before he vanished through an impossibly small hole in the skirting board, at which point the cat deigned to wake up and stretch luxuriantly. In my search for my prey I opened drawers that hadn't been opened for some time, revealing my favourite glasses cleaning cloth, shredded into bedding and shaped into a cosy nest.

I had been made a laughing stock and my revenge was fast and effective (thanks to B&Q), with 12 of the invaders dead within days and my nuts secured beneath a tight fitting lid. My wife kindly refrained from gloating.

"Everyone says it would make a great movie"

So often people decide they want to write a book because what they actually want to do is make a film. Who wouldn't prefer to have their story up in lights over Leicester Square rather than sitting on a table in Waterstones with a hundred other stories? Think of the premieres, the hanging out with film stars and the courting by the Hollywood executives.

It is a wonderful dream and anyone who investigates it will soon be told that it would be better to start with a book and then sell the rights, since every man, woman and both their dogs is trying to flog scripts to Hollywood, Bollywood and the BBC, and other outlets far too numerous to mention. That is when they start looking around for a ghostwriter to get them started.

"Someone in Hollywood wants to buy an option," is indeed a heart-warming message to get from an agent or publisher. It leads to a heady rush of euphoria, and sometimes a reasonable, but never life-changing, payment. The option is usually for six months or a year and is merely an agreement that you will not allow any other film or television company to buy the rights during that period. The producer then does their best to raise the money to make the film. One year is almost never long enough and they then have to decide if they want to renew the option.

Raising the money to make a film is a lot harder than raising the money to publish a book (which is now even cheaper thanks to digital publishing). A film crew and cast always cost hundreds of thousands of pounds, often millions, so the chances of any producer pulling it off in a year are always gossamer thin.

Despite the odds stacked against them, however, people continue to dream of becoming film producers, just as they dream of becoming authors. We all continue to hope that our latest project will be the one that will take off and become the next James Bond or Harry Potter, and in the meantime we keep on selling the film options year after year and enjoying ludicrously optimistic meetings in the sunshine of Los Angeles or the buzzing back streets of Soho, where famous names are bandied about as potential directors and stars before the money has even been raised or the script written.

I have literally lost count of the number of different producers and film companies who have bought options for *Sold* over the last 20 years. They have been based in London, Tel Aviv, Los Angeles and virtually every city in between and all of them share the same glowing optimism when they first take up the option, certain that they will be the ones who manage to bring it to fruition. Sometimes they give up after six months, sometimes they hang on in for a few years, renewing every few months, always certain that they are just about to pull the whole deal together and start shooting if they could just be given a little more time. Everything from getting a book published to getting a movie made always takes longer than anyone ever expects. We all need to be given a little more time.

Having said that, of course, all the world's most successful projects also started with the same mixture of hope and delusion. No one is ever going to win the lottery if they don't buy a ticket.

The strange delusions
of world leaders

It's a funny old thing, power. If someone has spent any number of years running a country or a giant corporation, coming to the end of your reign inevitably sends you a little bit mad.

To be honest, the madness probably takes root while they are still in power, when they are surrounded by yes-men and flatterers who never point out when they are being delusional, or just plain odd. I'm told by those who know about these things that eight years is probably the longest that you can hold high office before you start to lose touch with reality.

One of the first things they find when they return to the real world is that time hangs pretty heavy once they are out of office. If you're used to having every moment of your day scheduled and overseen by a crack team of assistants and advisers it must be disorienting to wake up and realise that if you want the day to be interesting you are going to have to make it happen yourself. There must also be a terrible realisation of their own mortality. "Is that it?" the ex-world leaders must think to themselves. "Are my best years now behind me?"

Almost certainly the answer to that is "yes". No matter how much money they accrue on the lecture circuit or how many charitable causes they make happen, nothing will ever quite match the moment of being voted President or Prime Minister of any country in the world. No matter how many billions you may find you have control of, nothing will match the excitement of starting your own bank against the odds somewhere dangerous in the developing world, and seeing it rise up the ranks of global institutions.

So in their early days out of power, when they are still trying to work out who they are and what they are going to do with their remaining days on the planet, these people often think that they will write a book. They want to "set the record straight" and they also want to make some money while their names are still recognised by at least a proportion of the paying public.

They are not always the easiest of people to deal with in those early post-power days. They are still used to getting everything they want the moment they want it, summoning people to their presence whatever the time or whatever the day. Some of them go a little wild with the freedom of being out of office — a bit like kids on the first day of the school holidays. In some cases that can mean that the ghostwriter is bombarded with unrealistic deadlines and other demands (I had one such client who required me to read the whole manuscript out loud to him because he was having trouble concentrating on the written words), and it can also mean that the ghost has to compete for the client's attention with other distractions, such as expensive Russian hookers. I find it is always a good idea to have a book with you if you are going to have to wait for your client to finish off in the bedroom before gracing you with his full(ish) attention.

It is usually a few years before they start to behave anything like normal people with normal expectations, perhaps regaining some of the charm and vision that first catapulted them to success.

Authors regain a little self-control

The explosion of self-publishing in the twenty-first century took everyone by surprise, particularly the existing publishers. It was one of those things that we didn't know we wanted until we had it — like televisions and mobile phones. In some ways, however, it is merely a small move back towards the fundamentals of being a storyteller.

In the beginning there were only storytellers and the people who made up their audiences as they moved from town to town, village to village. Then the storytellers learned to write and the audiences learned to read.

Next came the middlemen offering bags of gold and countless ideas on how to bring these two sets of people together more effectively. Some offered to print the words, design covers and transport the results to the audiences. Others offered to open shops where the stories could be displayed and promised they would be able to ensure that the stories were talked about and praised by all the right people.

Then they offered the possibilities of dramatising the most favoured stories on stages and screens, building cinemas and theatres for the audiences to come to and inventing radios and televisions which would carry the stories into people's homes.

All these services that the middlemen were offering were so useful to the storytellers and to their audiences that both became lazy, willing to allow the middlemen to do all the hard and boring work on their behalf, leaving themselves free to stay home and do the things they liked the best — writing, reading, watching and listening.

The middlemen grew increasingly powerful and soon the storytellers were more worried about pleasing them than they were about pleasing their audiences. The business people became the ones who decided what stories would and would not be told.

The storytellers spent all their energies trying to impress the middlemen and trying to persuade them to help. Those who failed to do so grew despondent and bitter. Then, when the publishers became too busy to read everything that was sent to them, the storytellers had to turn their attention to pleasing the agents who sprang up to serve the publishers.

And so it had come to pass that it was now the poor storytellers who were offering their services to the middlemen rather than the other way round, and the audiences could only gain access to the stories that had been blessed by those middlemen.

A lot of people were able to make a lot of money, of course, because that is what the middlemen are particularly good at, but this was not the way that things were meant to be when the storytellers first started and they began to feel ill at ease.

Then one day, in a dazzling flash of light, the internet appeared in everyone's lives and suddenly the middlemen with all their bags of gold didn't seem so important. Their services did not seem quite as useful because the storytellers found that with a little more effort, and without having to leave their homes, they could go straight to their audiences again, using a service which seemed to be almost as free and open as the country roads they had strolled along before the middlemen first arrived. Self-publishing, which had been damned as mere vanity during the reign of the middlemen, suddenly seemed a perfectly reasonable way to lay your goods out for the public to view.

Within a very short time most authors had learned how to publish themselves, or knew someone who could do it for them. Then came another development: the pop-up bookshop. Some of the authors who found it impossible to get their wares into the established retailers simply set up their own pop-up shops in premises that had been rendered dark by the high street crisis.

Whenever authors get together we can be heard complaining about those who we work alongside. We complain that our agents never return our calls; our publishers never promote our books and the booksellers then refuse to display them with the prominence they deserve.

Digital publishing called our bluff on the first two because we can now publish and promote our own stuff, so we have no one to blame but ourselves if things don't go as well as they did in our dreams. With pop-up shops any author who thought they could do better than Waterstones now has a chance to put their money where their mouth is.

If authors can be their own agents and their own publishers and their own booksellers we will never be able to complain about anything ever again — apart from the readers, of course, and no author ever complains about their readers, only the lack of them.

Standing on the past

The Southeast Branch of the Society of Authors was trying its hand at a pop-up bookshop for members in the Tunbridge Wells area.

It wasn't until I showed up at the mighty shopping mall that was going to be housing the shop, that I realised it was squatting on the site of my first holiday job as a scenery painter for the town's summer repertory company. My mother had seen an article about the place in the local paper while I was at school and had managed to wangle me a temporary apprenticeship.

I must have been 15 because I hadn't yet been presented with a scooter for my sixteenth birthday and had to catch the bus in each day from the village where my parents lived to a back-street laundry that had been converted into a theatre workshop.

I was apprenticed to an entertaining but world-weary Scottish designer, who would disappear from the workshop virtually as soon as the pubs opened, leaving me to happily munch my sandwiches amongst the scenery, props and costumes, dreaming of becoming a future Shakespeare, Wilde, Coward, Stoppard, or whoever was holding my imagination at the time, until closing time.

Forty-five years later I was back, inside the shopping mall that had crushed all the small streets of the area, including that one with the converted laundry, watching thousands of shoppers bustling around on top of my past. At the entrance to the mall a woman in costume was handing out flyers for the Christmas pantomime being staged at the same theatre I had helped paint scenery for.

The creation of Steffi McBride

One of my daughters was at drama school and I understood enough about the acting business to know that when she left she would be entering one of the most difficult and crowded professions in the world — offering even more opportunities for heartbreak than trying to write for a living.

In order to make a start she needed to have something that she could show to potential agents and casting directors. Every graduating drama student in the world would have photographs and all of them would be trying to persuade the gatekeepers of the industry that they deserved to be given a chance. She needed some sort of calling card which could be easily accessed, would show off her abilities and would stick in the memory of those who saw it.

It occurred to me that if I wrote a book which was narrated by a young girl breaking into show business and the celebrity world, I could ask my daughter to make a short film in the form of a monologue by the main character, which we could then post on YouTube as a promotion for the book, at the same time making it available and easily accessible at the touch of a button or two to anyone whom she might be approaching about possible representation or casting.

So, I conjured the character up in my head and ghostwrote for her in much the same way as I would have done if she had been one of the real-life actresses or celebrities I had worked with over the years. The result, *The Overnight Fame of Steffi McBride*, is the tale of a young girl who is talent-spotted at a local drama class by the casting director of the country's biggest soap opera and is catapulted into the tawdry world of modern celebrity. Once she is famous family skeletons emerge from the shadows, providing the dramatic tension and surprises needed to keep the plot rolling along.

The book was agented by Barbara Levy and published by John Blake, with my daughter's picture on the cover, and the YouTube monologue worked as planned.

A year or two later I was approached by some freelance film producers wanting to make a pilot episode for television with my daughter in the lead role and it looked as if it was going to provide exactly the sort of break she needed. The producers then patiently embarked on several years of meetings, trying to raise money and gain distribution for their project. It takes so long, however, to raise the necessary money to make even a half hour television pilot, that by the time they were actually ready to film, my daughter had grown too old to play the part which had originally been written for her. Life for a freelance actress (and freelance film producers for that matter) is definitely even more of a bitch than life for a freelance writer.

Encouraged by the success of *Steffi* I persuaded the publisher to commission a prequel, *The Fabulous Dreams of Maggie de Beer*, which followed the earlier career of Steffi's mother, who just happened to be the same age as me and arrived in the same part of London at roughly the same time (she left home at 15 whereas I had waited another two years), her head filled with much the same dreams and delusions as mine; the writer's ego once again struggling to be free of its chains.

A gathering of ghosts

In amongst the queries from potential clients that arrive in my inbox every day, there are often letters from other writers who are searching for tips on how to become ghostwriters themselves.

I try my best to be helpful (and to tempt them to buy my own handbook on the subject), and if their query is related to finding an agent there are one or two whom I will recommend because I know that they use ghosts a lot and I also know that they respond quickly and helpfully to anyone who approaches them. Lack of response from people who should be perfectly capable of at least being polite is all too common and can be very wearing on the spirit for people who are already struggling with the difficulties of earning their living by writing.

As Halloween 2013 approached Andrew Lownie, one of these agents and a man whom I have worked with a lot over the years (and who also founded the Biographers' Club), announced he was going to throw a "ghosts' party".

Although I have from time to time met other ghostwriters individually or even in small groups, this was the first time I had heard of someone this well connected in the publishing business inviting a large number of us to congregate under one roof.

Lownie's house rests in a Dickensian street in Westminster, nestling close to the Abbey, the traditional burial place of British monarchs and the scene of all their coronations since 1066. It seemed a very suitable area for ghosts old and new to congregate. It was tucked well away from the loud, costumed revellers already weaving around Victoria Street and Parliament Square amongst the crowds of workers heading home.

By the time I arrived the elegant first floor reception rooms were already thronged with ghosts. There were some I had met but many more were physical incarnations of names that had merely passed through my email box over the years, appearing before me now in corporeal form for the first time.

What was unusual and heartening about the merry throng was that many of them were young, ambitious and excited by the jobs they were getting. Usually when any number of authors are gathered together in one place the average age of the room is startlingly high and the conversations are peppered with woeful tales of financial struggles, disappointed dreams and pessimism about the future of storytelling. This gathering of ghosts, however, was imbued with a surprisingly refreshing spirit.

Meeting the daughter of God

The email was very matter-of-fact. The sender was a well-established international business woman. She was passing through London and would like to meet up for a chat about a possible book. Almost as an aside, she mentioned that she was the daughter of God.

I did a bit of googling, as I now do whenever I get an approach out of the blue, and there was plenty to read about her business career, although nothing about her unusual parentage. I was not the first person she had told about it, but this was going to be the first time she had considered stepping out into the public spotlight.

She was staying at the Four Seasons Hotel at the bottom of Park Lane (the same establishment in which billionaire Howard Hughes spent many of his final and most reclusive years, at which time it was called Inn on the Park) and asked if I would like to join her for lunch.

There seemed two possibilities here. Either she was mistaken about who her real father was or her birth was the most important thing to happen in the world for a couple of millennia. I decided it was worth investigating further. If she had invited me to talk about a business book I would have gone, so this possible extra

294

dimension to the story did not seem a good reason to refuse to listen to her.

The lunch was good. The lady was charming and entirely sincere in her beliefs, but in the end she decided that the time was not yet right to "come out" to the world. Maybe she will change her mind again later. I hope so. It would be a fun book to write.

My father's departure by tractor

Darkness had descended on the garden and I noticed that my father's windows still stood open. Normally by that time he would have come inside to administer the daily ritual of afternoon tea.

He and my mother had come to live with us in a self-contained flat some 10 years before. My mother had passed quietly away after a couple of years leaving my father to become a fixture in the lives of his grandchildren, always to be found working somewhere in the garden during the day, or in his sitting room in the evenings, pleased to receive their company.

From my office window I could see that his car was in the garage, so I knew he had not gone out. Arming myself with a torch I set out to investigate.

He had always joked that he would be happy to die on his tractor lawnmower — a sort of British version of Don Vito Corleone keeling over in his garden while playing with his grandson. I believe Vito's last words in the novel were, "Life is so beautiful."

And there I found my father, sitting on the tractor in its shed, struck down by his heart in just the same manner as Vito, exactly the end he had hoped for. Life can indeed be beautiful.

And still I know nothing

In his seminal book *Adventures in the Screen Trade*, Hollywood scriptwriter William Goldman famously came up with the phrase "nobody knows anything". His contention was that no one could predict which films would become blockbusters and which ones would flop hideously and expensively, no matter how experienced they were in the industry.

I guess the same is true in most professions and most walks of life, but I know for sure it is true in book publishing. For more than 40 years I have been taking stories to publishers and have been constantly surprised by the ones they would turn down and the ones that they would get into a bidding frenzy over in their desperation to buy. Once the books are published I am still repeatedly shocked by which ones the reading public take to their hearts and recommend to their friends and which ones sink without trace from the day of publication.

The only thing I know is that if you want to make a living from writing you have to keep producing work on a daily basis and you have to keep trying new things. If one project in 10 does all right and one in a hundred becomes a monster hit you may be okay, but you will never be able to predict which ones they are going to be.

The joy of self-publishing and the developments which Amazon and other technical pioneers have made possible mean that it is now easier to get a hundred projects up and running, no longer being dependent on the whims of publishers to even get into print, but still you can't predict which of the millions of books being produced is going to turn out to be *Fifty Shades of Grey*, the fastest selling book of all time. Nobody knew that was going to happen, any more than they realised that Ian Fleming and J. K. Rowling had created cultural icons that would become known throughout the world, growing into billion dollar businesses. I doubt if either Shakespeare or Dickens would ever have believed you if you'd told them how widely their writings would still be being read and performed centuries after the work of their contemporaries was largely forgotten.

Perhaps that uncertainty is one of the reasons that make writing and publishing such interesting professions.

Acknowledgements

With unbounded thanks to all the publishers, editors, agents, clients and readers who have helped to provide the raw material for these tales.

Other titles published by Ulverscroft:

BETRAYED

Lyndsey Harris & Andrew Crofts

A mother. A daughter. A family torn apart.

Until the age of six, Sarah Harris was a normal happy little girl. But then her life became a living hell — as she became the victim of a hate campaign. Before long she was suspended from school, alienated from her friends and utterly terrified.

For her mother, Lyndsey, it was a life beyond her worst nightmares. Her marriage was soon on the verge of collapse, then social services stepped in and suddenly Lyndsey was fighting to keep her family together — and to save her daughter's sanity. But worse was to come as Lyndsey discovered her family had been victims of the most hurtful betrayal of all.

LEAVING BEFORE THE RAINS COME

Alexandra Fuller

A child of the Rhodesian wars and daughter of two deeply complicated parents, Alexandra Fuller is no stranger to pain. But the disintegration of her own marriage leaves her shattered. Looking to pick up the pieces of her life, she finally confronts tough questions about her past, about the American man she married, and about the family she left behind in Africa. From her unusual courtship in Zambia — elephant attacks on the first date, sick with malaria on the wedding day — to the mountains of Wyoming, Fuller attempts to understand her younger self as she charts twenty years of her tempestuous marriage to the love of her life.

ONE WILD SONG

Paul Heiney

By the age of twenty-one, my son had sailed aboard a tall ship across the Atlantic and Pacific Oceans. At the age of twenty-two he wrote a poem which, once heard, can never be forgotten. At the age of twenty-three, he took his own life. This is what I did next . . . Cape Horn is renowned as one of the most remote and bleak parts of the world: the sailor's Everest. Paul Heiney set off from England — alone — to rediscover his son's voice through the medium of sailing, which Nicholas loved, and through the poignant poem that was his son's legacy. This is a story of adventurous seafaring, and of a man coming to terms with the greatest loss imaginable.

THE HOUSE IS FULL OF YOGIS

Will Hodgkinson

Once upon a time in the 1980s, the Hodgkinsons were just like any other family. Nev, Liz, Tom and Will lived the suburban dream. That is, until a questionable buffet gave Nev a bout of food poisoning which brought about a revelation. Their lives would never be the same again. Out went drunken dinner parties; in came hordes of white-clad Yogis meditating in the living room. While Tom took it all in his stride, the arrival of the Brahma Kumaris threw Will into crisis. As if that weren't enough, he also fell hopelessly in love with his best friend's sister . . .